BY THE EDITORS OF CONSUMER GUIDE®

Italian
COOKING CLASS
COOKBOOK

Contents

American edition produced under copyright by permission of *The
Australian Women's Weekly*, Sydney, Australia.

Manufactured in the United States of America
10 9 8 7 6 5 4 3

Library of Congress Catalog Card Number: 82-82131

ISBN: 0-517-38115X

Cover food stylist: Gail Klatt
Cover photography: Walter Gray

On the front cover: Summer Spaghetti and Antipasto
On the back cover: Ricotta Cake, Vegetable Salad,
                  and Amaretti

Introduction

Is any food as heartwarming as Italian food? Most of us develop a craving for this varied and delicious cuisine with our first taste of pasta. But the cooking secrets of a foreign cuisine don't always come naturally. That's why cooking classes devoted to Italian food have become so popular. With the **Italian Cooking Class Cookbook,** there is no need to attend a special cooking class—you've brought one right into your own kitchen.

Feel confident because the recipes in this book are designed to ensure your success. Every recipe has been thoughtfully formulated and kitchen tested to assure delicious results, and each is presented with complete, concise, step-by-step instructions. Each recipe is illustrated with a full-color photograph so that you can visualize the completed dish. In addition, most recipes also feature extra photographs to highlight helpful preparation techniques.

Italian Cooking Class Cookbook presents a representative cross section of some of the best specialties from the various provinces of Italy. An understanding of the Italian style of dining will unlock the secrets of Italian menu-making, and help you use this book to its greatest potential.

A true Italian meal is very different from the single, large plate of pasta most of us think of when we think "Italian." Pasta is, of course, included in an authentic Italian meal; but it is set apart in a separate course just before the main dish. The order of courses in an authentic Italian meal goes something like this:

Antipasto: a colorful, varied appetizer course.
I Primi: a normally delicate portion of pasta, risotto or gnocchi, or sometimes a soup.
I Secondi: the main course, featuring meat, fish or poultry.
Insalata: the salad course, usually featuring a tart, zesty salad or vegetable.
I Dolci: the dessert course, normally accompanied by coffee.

The word *antipasto* literally translated means "before the pasta." This course need not be limited to only those dishes called "appetizers"—it is really a mix 'n match extravaganza. For instance, the cool, white rings of Marinated Calamari, or a scaled-down portion of Vitello Tonnato, or even the cheese-stuffed Rice Croquettes would make wonderful antipasto.

Following the colorful antipasto course comes the course Italians call *I Primi*—the first things. Very often, *I Primi* consists of pasta, but served in small portions. Italians always cook pasta *al dente,* which literally translates as "to the tooth." This means the pasta has not been overcooked to a mushy, sodden state. It has a bit of firmness or "bite" remaining in it. Al dente pasta is a chewy, satisfying food. Differently shaped pastas cook in different lengths of time. For instance, the short, fat, corkscrew shape of rotelle may take longer to cook than slender strands of spaghetti.

The best way to cook pasta al dente is to start with plenty of boiling salted water. Use about 1 tablespoon salt (15 mL) to 4 quarts (4 L) water. You can also add 1 tablespoon (15 mL) of butter or oil to the water to prevent the pasta from sticking. Cook pasta, stirring occasionally, for 5 minutes; then begin testing it for doneness. Remove a piece and bite it or pinch between thumb and forefinger. When pasta is tender but firm, and to your liking, drain it. Serve pasta immediately or toss with a small amount of butter or oil to prevent sticking. Use oil if the accompanying sauce is robust and oil based. Choose butter if your sauce is light and buttery. Pasta is a favorite main dish in the United States, and served with a salad, Italian bread, coffee and a light dessert—what could be better!

In contrast to al dente pasta, the Italians prefer their rice very soft and creamy. These rice preparations are called risottos; a perfect example is Risotto Milanese. Just as with pasta, a risotto may be served alone as the *I Primi* course before the main dish.

Another possibility for the *I Primi* course are gnocchi. They are cousins of pasta—luscious dumpling pastas. Gnocchi come in many forms. Gnocchi alla Romana, for example, are made with a special type of flour called semolina. Semolina is a meal made from a particular type of wheat and is milled in two styles. The first is a coarse grind which has the grainy consistency of fine sand; it is cooked like a cereal. This type is used in Gnocchi alla Romana. The second type of semolina is a very fine powder; it feels and looks like a yellowish version of regular flour. This finely ground semolina is often used for pasta making.

Italian soups can be hale and hearty—good enough to make meals in themselves; or they can be light and gracious—perfect *I Primi* courses in a longer meal.

Next, come the pleasures of the Italian main course. Called *I Secondi,* the second things, it features the best and freshest in meats, poultry and fish. In Italian cuisine, veal is a favorite meat and is often pounded very thin for quick sautéeing. To pound cutlets, lay them on a board or counter, cover with a sheet of waxed paper, and pound firmly with a broad, flat implement. The flat of a broad knife or cleaver, the clean back of a small pan, or the edges of a heavy plate may be used to pound veal to the specified thickness.

In an Italian meal, the salad course follows the main meat or fish dishes. Called *Insalata,* this course is served after the main course to perk up tired tastebuds.

Once refreshed by the salad course, the Italians are ready for their desserts, called *I Dolci*—the sweets. Candied peels or glacéed fruits are very popular ingredients in Italian desserts. There is really not much difference between the two items, except that whole or large chunks of fruit—such as cherries or pineapple rings—are often called glacéed, while fine diced peels are usually called candied.

Appetizers

An antipasto should make a light and tempting start to the meal. Beyond that there are no set rules. It can be one simple dish, such as Frittata, Bagna Cauda, or any of the dishes included in this chapter. Or, it can consist of an assortment of delicatessen meats, marinated vegetables and salads, and fresh fruits, artfully displayed in colorful array on a platter. We have on our platter clockwise from marinated mushrooms: mortadella, smoked bacon, genoa salami overlapping with capicola, tongue; Center of platter: marinated artichoke hearts and olives, roasted red peppers, prosciutto and melon.

Antipasto

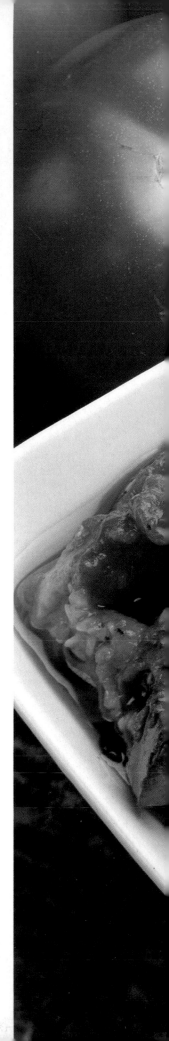

Eggplant Appetizer

3 large ripe tomatoes
3 medium cloves garlic
2 pounds (900 g) eggplant
 (2 medium)
1 cup (250 mL) olive oil
¾ teaspoon (4 mL) dried
 basil, crumbled
½ teaspoon (2 mL) dried
 oregano, crumbled
½ cup (125 mL) water
1 tablespoon (15 mL) tomato
 paste
1½ teaspoons (7 mL) salt
¼ teaspoon (1 mL) pepper

1. Place tomatoes in large saucepan with boiling water to cover, 60 seconds to loosen skins. Immediately drain tomatoes and rinse under cold running water. Peel, seed and chop tomatoes; reserve. Mince garlic; reserve.

2. Rinse eggplant; cut lengthwise into ½-inch- (1.5 cm) thick slices. Cut slices crosswise in half; then cut lengthwise into ½-inch- (1.5 cm) wide sticks.

3. Heat oil in large skillet over medium-high heat. Add half the eggplant to skillet; cook and stir 5 minutes. Remove eggplant with slotted spoon, draining well, to plate or bowl. Add remaining eggplant to oil remaining in skillet; cook and stir 5 minutes. Remove eggplant with slotted spoon to plate or bowl.

4. If there is no oil remaining in skillet, press eggplant with back of spoon to extract at least 2 tablespoons (30 mL) oil and place oil in skillet. Add reserved garlic, the basil and oregano to skillet; sauté over medium heat 30 seconds. Stir in reserved tomatoes, the water, tomato paste, salt and pepper. Simmer uncovered, stirring occasionally, 5 minutes. Stir eggplant into sauce. Cook and stir over low heat until thick, about 5 minutes longer. Serve hot or at room temperature.

**Makes about 6 cups (1.5 L);
10 to 12 servings.**

Vegetable Pickles

¼ head cauliflower
6 small white onions
2 large carrots
1 large red bell pepper
1 medium cucumber
2½ cups (625 mL) red or
    white wine vinegar
¼ cup (60 mL) sugar
1½ teaspoons (7 mL) whole
    mustard seeds
1 teaspoon (5 mL) whole
    celery seeds
¾ teaspoon (4 mL) salt
12 whole peppercorns
1 small whole dried hot red
    chili pepper

1. Place 2 clean heatproof pint (500 mL) jars and their lids in kettle with water to cover. Heat to boiling; boil 15 minutes. Turn off heat; leave jars in water until ready to fill.

2. Cut cauliflower into bite-size flowerets. Peel onions. Pare carrots; cut lengthwise into ⅛-inch- (0.5 cm) thick slices; cut slices crosswise in thirds. Core and seed bell pepper; cut into large chunks. Cut cucumber lengthwise into 4 wedges; cut out and discard seeds. Cut cucumber wedges lengthwise in half, then crosswise in thirds.

3. Place cauliflower, onions and carrots in large saucepan of boiling water. Cook 2 minutes; drain well.

4. Combine cauliflower, onions, carrots, bell pepper and cucumber in medium bowl; mix lightly. Drain hot sterilized jars; fill with vegetable mixture, leaving 1-inch (2.5 cm) headspace between the vegetables and top of the jar.

5. Measure vinegar, sugar, mustard and celery seeds, salt, peppercorns and chili pepper into small saucepan. Heat to boiling; boil 30 seconds. Remove from heat. Remove and discard chili pepper.

6. Immediately pour hot vinegar mixture into jars, covering vegetables and leaving ½-inch (1.5 cm) headspace between the liquid and the top of the jar. Cover jars securely with lids. Let stand on wire rack until completely cool. Refrigerate at least 1 week to mellow flavors before serving. Pickles will keep several weeks in refrigerator. Serve pickles as a relish or as part of an antipasto tray.

Makes 2 pints (1 L).

Marinated Mushrooms

3 tablespoons (45 mL) fresh
    lemon juice
2 tablespoons (30 mL)
    chopped fresh parsley
½ teaspoon (2 mL) salt
¼ teaspoon (1 mL) dried
    tarragon, crumbled
⅛ teaspoon (0.5 mL) pepper
½ cup (125 mL) olive oil
1 large clove garlic
½ pound (225 g) small fresh
    mushrooms

1. To make marinade, combine lemon juice, parsley, salt, tarragon and pepper in medium bowl. Whisking continuously, add oil in slow steady stream; whisk until oil is thoroughly blended. Lightly crush garlic with flat side of chef's knife or with mallet. Spear garlic with small wooden pick and add to marinade.

2. Break stems off mushrooms; reserve stems for another use. Wipe mushroom caps clean with damp kitchen towel; cut caps into thin slices. Add mushroom slices to marinade; stir to mix well. Marinate mushrooms covered, stirring occasionally, 4 hours at room temperature or overnight in refrigerator.

3. Remove and discard garlic before serving. Serve mushrooms as a relish or as part of an antipasto tray. Or, add mushrooms to tossed green salad, using the marinade as the dressing.

**Makes about 2 cups
(500 mL); 6 to 8 servings.**

Frittata

¼ cup (60 mL) olive oil
5 small yellow onions, thinly
sliced
1 can (14½ ounces or 415 g)
whole peeled tomatoes,
drained and chopped
¼ pound (115 g) smoked
ham, chopped
¼ cup (60 mL) grated
Parmesan cheese
2 tablespoons (30 mL)
minced fresh parsley
½ teaspoon (2 mL) dried
marjoram, crumbled
¼ teaspoon (1 mL) dried
basil, crumbled
¼ teaspoon (1 mL) salt
Large pinch pepper
6 large eggs
2 tablespoons (30 mL) butter

1. Heat oil in medium skillet over medium-high heat. Add onions; cook, stirring frequently, until onions are golden brown, 6 to 8 minutes. Drain chopped tomatoes and stir into onions; cook over medium heat, stirring constantly, 5 minutes. Remove tomatoes and onions from skillet to large bowl with slotted spoon; discard drippings. Let tomato-onion mixture cool to room temperature.

2. Add ham, cheese, parsley, marjoram, basil, salt and pepper to cooled tomato-onion mixture; mix lightly. Whisk eggs in small bowl; stir into ham mixture.

3. Heat broiler. Heat butter over medium heat in 10-inch (25 cm) heavy skillet with flameproof handle; when foam subsides, reduce heat to very low.

4. Add egg mixture to skillet; spread in even layer. Cook without stirring over very low heat until all but top ¼-inch (0.5 cm) of egg mixture is set, to 10 minutes; shake pan gently to test. Place skillet under broiler, about 4 inches (10 cm) from heat; cook just until top of egg mixture is set, to 2 minutes. Do not let top brown or frittata will be dry. Frittata can be served hot, room temperature or cold.

Makes 6 to 8 appetizer or 3 to 4 luncheon servings.

Crostini

12 slices firm white bread
5 tablespoons (75 mL) butter
2 tablespoons (30 mL)
all-purpose flour
½ cup (125 mL) milk
3 ounces (85 g) fresh
mushrooms (about 9
medium), finely chopped
6 tablespoons (90 mL) grated
Parmesan cheese
2 teaspoons (10 mL) anchovy
paste
¼ teaspoon (1 mL) salt
⅛ teaspoon (0.5 mL) pepper
Green and ripe olive halves;
red and green bell pepper
strips; rolled anchovy
fillets

1. Heat oven to 350°F (180°C). Cut circles out of bread slices with 2-inch (5 cm) round cutter. Melt 3 tablespoons (45 mL) of the butter in a small saucepan. Brush both sides of bread circles lightly with butter. Bake bread circles on ungreased baking sheet, turning circles over once, until golden, 5 to 6 minutes per side. Cool on wire rack. Do not turn oven off; increase setting to 425°F (220°C).

2. Melt remaining 2 tablespoons (30 mL) butter in small saucepan. Stir in flour; cook and stir over medium heat until bubbly. Whisk in milk; cook, stirring constantly, until sauce thickens and bubbles for 1 minute. Sauce will be very thick. Stir sauce into mushrooms in large bowl; stir in 3 tablespoons (45 mL) of the cheese, the anchovy paste, salt and pepper.

3. Spread a heaping teaspoon of mushroom mixture on top of each toast round; place on ungreased baking sheet. Sprinkle remaining 3 tablespoons (45 mL) cheese over crostini, dividing evenly. Decorate with olive halves, pepper strips, or rolled anchovy fillets. Bake until tops are light brown, 5 to 7 minutes. Serve hot.

Makes 2 to 2½ dozen crostini; 8 to 10 servings.

Sicilian Caponata

1½ pounds (675 g) eggplant (about 1 large or 2 small)
1 tablespoon (15 mL) salt
2 large red bell peppers
1 large onion
1 large stalk celery
¼ cup (60 mL) olive oil
⅛ to ¼ teaspoon (0.5 to 1 mL) dried hot red pepper flakes
1 can (14½ ounces or 415 g) whole peeled tomatoes
1 large clove garlic
2 tablespoons (30 mL) red wine vinegar
1 tablespoon (15 mL) sugar
8 Italian- or Greek-style black olives
1 tablespoon (15 mL) drained capers

1. Rinse eggplant; cut into ¾-inch (2 cm) cubes. Place in large colander; sprinkle with salt and toss. Let stand and drain in sink or over bowl, tossing occasionally, 1 hour. Rinse eggplant and drain well; squeeze in clean kitchen towel to extract moisture. Reserve.

2. Core and seed bell peppers; cut into ¾-inch (2 cm) chunks. Chop onion coarsely. Cut celery diagonally into ¼-inch- (0.5 cm) thick slices.

3. Heat oil in 10-inch (25 cm) noncorrosive skillet over medium-high heat. Add bell peppers, onion, celery and pepper flakes; sauté 5 minutes. Add reserved eggplant; cook over medium heat, stirring occasionally, 5 minutes longer. Remove from heat.

4. Press tomatoes and their liquid through sieve into vegetables in skillet; discard seeds. Mince garlic; add garlic to skillet. Stir in vinegar and sugar. Cook and stir over medium-high heat 3 minutes. Remove from heat.

5. Pit and chop olives. Add olives and capers to skillet. Cook over medium-low heat, stirring occasionally, until most of the liquid has evaporated and sauce is thickened, about 10 minutes. Serve hot as a vegetable sidedish; or, cool to room temperature and serve as a relish or on an antipasto tray.

Makes about 5 cups (1.25 L); 8 to 10 servings.

Bagna Cauda

Assorted fresh vegetables such as mushrooms, green and red bell peppers, celery, cauliflower, tomatoes, carrots, cucumbers and green onions
1 pint (500 mL) whipping cream
2 medium cloves garlic
6 to 8 flat anchovy fillets
¼ cup (60 mL) unsalted butter
Thinly sliced Italian bread

1. Clean and trim vegetables; cut into bite-size pieces. You should have a total of 6 cups (1.5 L) prepared vegetables. Place in small dishes or arrange attractively on serving tray. Cover with damp paper towels, then with plastic wrap. Refrigerate until serving time.

2. Heat cream in large heavy saucepan over medium heat just to boiling; reduce heat to medium-low. Cook, stirring occasionally, until cream is reduced and measures 1 cup (250 mL), about 20 minutes.

3. Meanwhile, mince garlic. Drain anchovies and pat dry with paper towels; chop very fine.

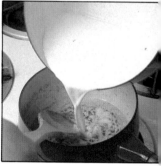

4. Melt butter in small heavy saucepan over low heat; do not let butter brown. Add garlic and anchovies. Cook and stir, mashing anchovies with back of spoon, until ingredients are blended and form a thin paste.

5. Stirring butter mixture continuously, add cream in slow steady stream. Cook and stir over low heat just until sauce is smooth and hot; do not boil. Serve sauce at once with prepared vegetables and bread. (Note: To eat, each guest dips vegetables into sauce and uses bread to catch the drippings.)

Makes 4 to 6 servings.

Soups

Minestrone

3 medium carrots
3 stalks celery
2 medium onions
1 large potato
¼ pound (115 g) green beans
2 medium zucchini
½ pound (225 g) cabbage
1 medium clove garlic
⅓ cup (80 mL) olive oil
3 tablespoons (45 mL) butter
3½ cups (825 mL) beef broth
1½ cups (375 mL) water
1 can (28 ounces or 790 g)
    Italian plum tomatoes
½ teaspoon (2 mL) each salt
    and dried basil, crumbled
¼ teaspoon (1 mL) each
    pepper and dried
    rosemary, crumbled
1 bay leaf
1 can (1 pound or 450 g)
    cannellini beans

1. Pare carrots; chop coarsely. Chop celery coarsely. Chop onions. Pare potato; cut into ¾-inch (2 cm) cubes. Trim green beans; cut into 1-inch (2.5 cm) pieces. Trim zucchini; cut into ½-inch (1.5 cm) cubes. Coarsely shred cabbage. Mince garlic.

2. Heat oil and butter in 5-quart (5 L) Dutch oven over medium heat. Add onions; sauté stirring occasionally, until soft and golden but not brown, 6 to 8 minutes. Stir in carrots and potato; sauté 5 minutes. Stir in celery and green beans; sauté 5 minutes. Stir in zucchini; sauté 3 min-

utes. Stir in cabbage and garlic; cook 1 minute.

3. Add broth, water and liquid from tomatoes to pan. Chop tomatoes coarsely; add to pan. Stir in salt, basil, rosemary, pepper and bay leaf. Heat to boiling; reduce heat to low. Simmer covered, stirring occasionally, 1½ hours.

4. Rinse and drain cannellini beans; add beans to soup. Cook uncovered over

medium-low heat, stirring occasionally, until soup is thick, 30 to 40 minutes longer. Remove bay leaf.

Makes about 12 cups (3 L); 8 to 10 servings.

Note: Soup can be served with grated Parmesan cheese to sprinkle, if desired.

Stracciatella

2 chicken thighs
2 stalks celery
1 large carrot, pared
1 large onion
6 cups (1.5 L) water
½ teaspoon (2 mL) whole
  peppercorns
3 large eggs
⅔ cup (160 mL) grated
  Parmesan cheese (about 2
  ounces or 60 g)
2 tablespoons (30 mL)
  chopped fresh parsley
Large pinch ground nutmeg
¼ teaspoon (1 mL) salt
Pinch pepper

1. To make stock: Rinse chicken thighs; place in small Dutch oven. Cut celery, carrot and onion into large chunks; add to Dutch oven. Add 6 cups (1.5 L) water and the peppercorns. Heat to boiling; reduce heat to low. Simmer covered 1 hour.

2. Strain stock through sieve lined with dampened cheesecloth into 3-quart (3 L) saucepan. Discard vegetables and peppercorns; reserve chicken for another use.

3. Degrease stock as follows. Let stock stand 5 minutes to allow fat to rise. Hold paper towel in both hands. Quickly pull towel across surface of stock; towel will absorb fat. Discard towel. Repeat with clean towels, as many times as needed to remove all fat. Skim surface only, without letting towel dip down into the stock itself.

4. Whisk eggs in small bowl until well beaten; whisk in cheese, parsley and nutmeg. Heat degreased stock over medium-high heat to boiling. Stir stock rapidly with spoon or whisk while adding egg mixture in thin steady stream. Immediately remove soup from heat. Let stand 2 minutes before serving. Season with salt and pepper just before serving.

**Makes about 6 cups (1.5 L);
4 to 6 servings.**

Meatball Soup

2 pounds (900 g) beef
  soupbones
3 stalks celery
2 carrots, pared
1 medium onion, cut in half
1 bay leaf
6 cups (1.5 L) cold water
1 tablespoon (15 mL) olive
  oil
1 large egg
4 tablespoons (60 mL)
  minced fresh parsley
1 teaspoon (5 mL) salt
½ teaspoon (2 mL) dried
  marjoram, crumbled
¼ teaspoon (1 mL) pepper
½ cup (125 mL) soft fresh
  breadcrumbs
¼ cup (60 mL) grated
  Parmesan cheese
1 pound (450 g) ground beef
  chuck
1 can (14½ ounces or 415 g)
  whole peeled tomatoes
½ cup (125 mL) uncooked
  small pasta

1. To make stock: Rinse bones; combine with celery, carrots, onion and bay leaf in small Dutch oven. Add 6 cups (1.5 L) water. Heat to boiling; reduce heat to low. Simmer 1 hour, partially covered, skimming foam occasionally.

2. Meanwhile, heat oven to 400°F (200°C). Spread oil in 13 × 9 × 2-inch (33 × 23 × 5 cm) baking pan. Combine egg, 3 tablespoons (45 mL) of the parsley, ½ teaspoon (2 mL) of the salt, the marjoram and ⅛ teaspoon (0.5 mL) of the pepper in medium bowl; whisk

lightly. Stir in breadcrumbs and cheese. Add beef; mix thoroughly with hands. Shape mixture into small balls, a heaping teaspoonful each; place in oiled pan. Bake meatballs, turning occasionally, until brown on all sides and cooked through, 20 to 25 minutes. Drain meatballs on paper toweling.

3. Strain stock through sieve into medium bowl. Slice carrots and celery; reserve. Discard bones, onion and bay leaf. Degrease stock; return stock to Dutch oven. Drain liq-

uid from tomatoes into stock. Chop tomatoes fine in can with scissors or knife; add to stock. Heat to boiling; boil uncovered 5 minutes. Stir in pasta and remaining salt and pepper. Cook uncovered over medium-high heat, stirring occasionally, 6 minutes. Add reserved vegetables and the meatballs. Cook uncovered over medium heat, stirring occasionally, 10 minutes. Stir in remaining parsley. Taste soup and adjust seasonings.

**Makes about 7 cups (1.75 L)
4 to 6 servings.**

Clam Soup

1 dozen hard-shell clams
3 cups (750 mL) plus 3 tablespoons (45 mL) water
1 large yellow onion, sliced
1 stalk celery, chopped
1 cup (250 mL) dry white wine
3 sprigs parsley
¼ teaspoon (1 mL) dried thyme
1 pound (450 g) red snapper, cod or striped bass fillets, skinned
6 ounces (170 g) fresh mushrooms, thinly sliced
5 green onions, thinly sliced
2 tablespoons (30 mL) olive oil
½ teaspoon (2 mL) salt
⅛ teaspoon (0.5 mL) pepper
⅛ to ¼ (0.5 to 1 mL) teaspoon hot red pepper sauce
1 tablespoon (15 mL) cornstarch
½ cup (125 mL) whipping cream

1. Scrub clams with stiff brush under cold running water. Soak clams in large basin of cold water 30 minutes. Lift out clams; discard water. Repeat soaking 2 more times.

2. Combine clams and 2 tablespoons (30 mL) of the water in large saucepan. Cook covered over medium heat just until clams open, 5 to 10 minutes. Check frequently and

remove clams as they open so they don't overcook. Discard any clams that fail to open. Strain clam broth through triple thickness of dampened cheesecloth; reserve. Rinse clams; reserve.

3. To make court bouillon: Combine yellow onion, celery, 3 cups (750 mL) of the water, the wine, parsley and thyme in medium noncorrosive saucepan. Heat to simmering. Simmer 30 minutes. Do not boil. Strain bouillon; discard solids. Combine fish fillets with bouillon in saucepan. Cook over low heat just until fish is opaque, about 5 minutes. Remove fish with slotted spoon to plate; reserve. Reserve bouillon.

4. Sauté mushrooms and green onions in oil in small noncorrosive Dutch oven over medium heat until mushrooms are tender, 4 to 5 minutes. Stir in reserved bouillon, reserved clam broth, the salt, pepper and pepper sauce. Mix cornstarch and remaining 1 tablespoon (15 mL) water in cup until smooth; stir into soup. Simmer over low heat, stirring frequently, 5 minutes. Remove from heat.

5. Flake reserved fish with fork; add to soup. Stir cream into soup. Remove half the clams from their shells and discard shells; add clams to soup. Add remaining clams, still in their shells, to soup. Heat over medium-low heat just until soup is hot; do not boil. Serve at once.

Makes about 7 cups (1.75 L); 4 to 6 servings.

Bean & Pasta Soup

1¼ cups (310 mL) dried navy (pea) beans
6 cups (1.5 L) cold water
3 strips bacon, finely chopped
1 large onion, finely chopped
1 large stalk celery, chopped
¾ pound (340 g) smoked pork rib or neck bones
2 medium cloves garlic, minced
½ teaspoon (2 mL) each dried thyme and marjoram, crumbled
¼ teaspoon (1 mL) pepper
¾ cup (180 mL) uncooked small pasta
2 tablespoons (30 mL) minced fresh parsley
Pinch salt
1 cup (250 mL) beef broth, if needed

1. Rinse and sort beans. Combine beans and 6 cups (1.5 L) water in large saucepan. Heat over high heat to boiling; boil uncovered 2 minutes. Remove from heat; let beans soak covered 1 hour. Do not drain.

2. Cook bacon in medium skillet over medium-high heat 2 minutes. Add onion and celery; sauté, stirring frequently, until vegetables are light brown, about 6 minutes. Remove bacon and vegetables with slotted spoon to plate; discard drippings. Rinse pork bones to remove excess salt; add bones to beans and soaking water in saucepan. Add sautéed bacon and vegetables.

Stir garlic, thyme, marjoram and pepper into bean mixture. Heat over high heat to boiling; reduce heat to low. Simmer covered, stirring occasionally, until beans are tender, about 1 hour. Remove from heat.

3. Remove bones from soup to plate; reserve. Remove about half the beans from soup with slotted spoon; puree these beans with 2 tablespoons (30 mL) soup liquid in blender or food processor. Stir puree into soup remaining in saucepan.

4. Heat soup to boiling. Stir in pasta; cook uncovered over medium heat, stirring occasionally, until pasta is tender, 8 to 12 minutes.

5. While pasta is cooking, remove meat from reserved bones; discard bones. Chop meat fine. Stir meat and parsley into soup just before serving. Taste soup; add salt if needed. Soup will thicken on standing; if necessary, stir in as much of the beef broth as needed to thin.

Makes about 6 cups (1.5 L); 6 servings.

Note: Soup can be served with grated Parmesan cheese to sprinkle if desired.

Lentil Soup

1¼ cups (310 mL) dried
  lentils
¾ pound (340 g) smoked
  pork rib or neck bones
1 large onion
1 large carrot
1 large stalk celery
2 tablespoons (30 mL) butter
1 tablespoon (15 mL) olive
  oil
2¼ cups (560 mL) water
1 can (14 ounces or 400 g)
  beef broth
1 to 2 tablespoons (15 to 30
  mL) red wine vinegar
1 can (14½ ounces or 415 g)
  whole peeled tomatoes
¼ teaspoon (1 mL) pepper
1 bay leaf
2 tablespoons (30 mL)
  minced fresh parsley
Pinch salt

1. Rinse and sort lentils; re-serve. Rinse bones to remove excess salt; reserve. Chop onion. Pare and dice carrot. Slice celery.

2. Heat butter and oil in 5-quart (5 L) Dutch oven over medium heat. Add onion, carrot and celery; sauté until onion is soft, about 6 minutes. Add reserved lentils and bones to pan. Stir in 2¼ cups (560 mL) water, the broth and 1 tablespoon (15 mL) of the vinegar. Drain liquid from tomatoes into pan. Finely chop tomatoes in can with scissors or knife; add to pan. Stir in pepper and bay leaf. Heat over high heat to boiling; reduce heat to low. Simmer covered, stirring occasionally, until lentils are tender, 50 to 60 minutes. Remove from heat.

3. Remove and discard ba[y] leaf. Remove bones from sou[p] to plate; let bones cool slightl[y.] Remove meat from bones; dis[-]card bones. Chop meat fine[;] stir into soup. Heat soup jus[t] to simmering; remove fro[m] heat. Stir in parsley. Taste sou[p] and add salt and remainin[g] vinegar if needed.

Makes about 9 cups (2.25 L)[.]
6 to 8 servings.

Fish Soup

6 to 8 hard-shell clams
1 quart (1 L) plus 2
  tablespoons (30 mL) water
1 cup (250 mL) dry white
  wine
2 onions, thinly sliced
1 stalk celery, chopped
3 sprigs parsley
1 bay leaf
¾ pound (340 g) ocean perch
  or snapper fillets
1 can (14½ ounces or 415 g)
  whole peeled tomatoes
1 tablespoon (15 mL) tomato
  paste
1 large clove garlic, minced
1 teaspoon (5 mL) dried
  oregano, crumbled
1 teaspoon (5 mL) salt
½ teaspoon (2 mL) sugar
⅛ teaspoon (0.5 mL) pepper
2 large ripe tomatoes
2 large potatoes
1 pound (450 g) fresh halibut
  or haddock fillets
½ pound (225 g) fresh
  medium shrimp in shells
2 tablespoons (30 mL)
  chopped fresh parsley

1. Scrub and soak clams as in
Clam Soup (page 16).

2. Combine 1 quart (1 L) of the water, the wine, onions, celery, parsley sprigs and bay leaf in 6-quart (6 L) noncorrosive stockpot. Heat to boiling; reduce heat to very low. Add perch; barely simmer uncovered 20 minutes.

3. Strain fish stock through sieve into bowl. Remove perch to plate; reserve. Discard other solids. Return stock to stockpot. Press canned tomatoes and their liquid through sieve into stockpot. Stir in tomato paste, garlic, oregano, salt, sugar and pepper. Simmer uncovered over medium-low heat 20 minutes.

4. Meanwhile, combine clams and remaining 2 tablespoons (30 mL) water in large saucepan. Cook covered over medium heat just until clams open, 5 to 10 minutes; remove clams immediately as they open. Discard any clams with unopened shells. Rinse clams; reserve.

5. Seed fresh tomatoes; chop coarsely. Pare potatoes; cut into ¾-inch (2 cm) cubes. Skin halibut; cut into 1½ x 1-inch (4 x 2.5 cm) pieces. Add fresh tomatoes, potatoes and halibut to stockpot. Heat to boiling; reduce heat to medium-

low. Cook covered until pota[-]toes are tender, 12 to 1[5] minutes.

6. Shell and devein shrimp[;] add to soup. Cook ove[r] medium heat just until shrim[p] are cooked through, 1 to 2 min[-]utes. Flake reserved perch; sti[r]

perch, reserved clams an[d] chopped parsley into soup[.] Serve immediately.

Makes about 10 cups (2.5 L)[.]
6 to 8 servings.

Pasta & Sauces

Tortellini with Creamed Mushroom Sauce

2 cups (500 mL) plus 1
   tablespoon (15 mL)
   all-purpose flour
½ teaspoon (2 mL) salt
4 large eggs
1 tablespoon (15 mL) milk
1 teaspoon (5 mL) olive oil
1 small cooked chicken
   breast, skinned, boned,
   and minced
2 ounces (60 g) fresh
   spinach, cleaned, cooked,
   squeezed very dry and
   minced
2 ounces (60 g) prosciutto,
   minced
⅓ cup (80 mL) plus 5
   tablespoons (75 mL)
   grated Parmesan cheese
2 cups (500 mL) whipping
   cream
Pinch pepper
½ pound (225 g) fresh
   mushrooms, thinly sliced
3 tablespoons (45 mL) butter
Boiling salted water
3 tablespoons (45 mL)
   chopped fresh parsley

1. Mix flour and ¼ teaspoon (1 mL) of the salt on board; make well in center. Whisk 3 of the eggs, the milk and oil in small bowl; gradually pour into well in flour while mixing with fingertips or a fork to form firm dough. Knead dough until smooth and elastic, about 5 minutes. Reserve dough, at room temperature, wrapped in plastic while making filling.

2. Combine chicken, spinach, prosciutto and the remaining egg in medium bowl; mix well. Add 2 tablespoons (30 mL) of the Parmesan cheese, 1 tablespoon (15 mL) of the cream, the remaining ¼ teaspoon (1 mL) salt and the pepper to spinach mixture; mix well.

3. Knead pasta dough briefly on lightly floured surface; divide dough in thirds. Roll out, cut and fill a third of dough at a time as follows; keep unused pieces and any scraps wrapped in plastic to prevent drying. Let dough rest 1 minute; then roll out on lightly floured surface until 1/16-inch (2 mm) or less thick. Cut out dough circles with 2-inch (5 cm) round cutter. Cover rolled dough with clean kitchen towel to prevent drying while you work. Place ½ teaspoon (2 mL) spinach filling

in center of a dough circle; brush edge of circle lightly with water. Fold circle in half to enclose filling; pinch outside edges together firmly to seal. Brush end of half-circle with water; wrap around finger, overlap ends, and pinch to seal. Place tortellini on clean kitchen towel. Repeat process until all filling has been used; dough scraps can be rerolled, cut, and filled if needed. Let tortellini dry on towel for 30 minutes before cooking.

4. Sauté mushrooms in butter in 3-quart (3 L) saucepan over medium heat 3 minutes. Stir in remaining cream. Heat to boiling; reduce heat to low. Simmer uncovered 3 minutes. Stir in ⅓ cup (80 mL) of the cheese; cook and stir 1 minute. Remove from heat.

5. Cook tortellini, a third at a time, in large pot of boiling salted water just until al dente, 2 to 3 minutes. Drain well; add to sauce. When all tortellini have been cooked, heat in sauce over medium heat to simmering. Reduce heat to low; simmer 2 minutes. Serve sprinkled with parsley and remaining cheese.

Makes 6 to 8 servings.

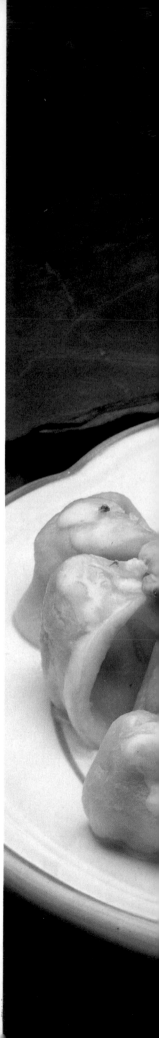

Rotelle with Spinach Sauce

10 ounces (285 g) fresh
  spinach
Warm salted water
¼ pound (115 g) coppa
  (Italian smoked pork)
1 small red or green bell
  pepper
1 small onion
1 medium clove garlic
1 small red or green hot chili
  pepper
8 ounces (225 g) uncooked
  spiral-shaped pasta, such
  as rotelle or rotini
Boiling salted water
6 tablespoons (90 mL) olive
  oil
3 tablespoons (45 mL) grated
  Parmesan cheese
½ teaspoon (2 mL) salt
⅛ teaspoon (0.5 mL) pepper
Grated Parmesan cheese, if
  desired

1. Rinse spinach thoroughly
in large basin of warm salted
water; drain well. Remove and

discard stems; cut spinach into
coarse shreds. Finely dice
coppa. Core, seed and dice bell
pepper. Finely chop onion.
Mince garlic. Seed and mince
chili pepper. (*Caution:* Chili
peppers can sting and irritate

skin; wear rubber gloves when
handling peppers and do not
touch eyes.)

2. Cook pasta in large saucepan boiling salted water just
until al dente, 8 to 12 minutes;
drain well.

3. While pasta is cooking, heat
oil in 10-inch (25 cm) skillet
over medium heat. Add
coppa, bell pepper, onion,
garlic and chili pepper; sauté 3
minutes. Add spinach; cook,
stirring constantly, 2 minutes
longer. Remove from heat.

4. Stir 3 tablespoons (45 mL)
cheese, the salt and pepper
into spinach mixture in skillet.
Combine with pasta in heated
serving bowl; toss well. Serve
immediately with extra cheese
to sprinkle.

Makes 4 servings.

Spaghetti Mediterranean

1½ pounds (675 g) fresh
  tomatoes (about 4 large)
12 pitted green olives
4 to 6 flat anchovy fillets
2 medium cloves garlic
½ pound (225 g) uncooked
  spaghetti
Boiling salted water
¼ cup (60 mL) olive oil
½ cup (125 mL) chopped
  fresh parsley
1 tablespoon (15 mL) drained
  capers
2 teaspoons (10 mL) chopped
  fresh basil or ½ teaspoon
  (2 mL) dried basil,
  crumbled
½ teaspoon (2 mL) dried
  oregano, crumbled
½ teaspoon (2 mL) salt
¼ teaspoon (1 mL) dried hot
  red pepper flakes

1. Place tomatoes in large
saucepan with boiling water to
cover, 60 seconds to loosen
skins. Immediately drain
tomatoes and rinse under cold
running water. Peel, seed and
chop tomatoes coarsely. Slice
olives. Chop anchovies. Crush
garlic through a press.

2. Cook spaghetti in large kettle of boiling salted water just
until al dente, 8 to 12 minutes;
drain well.

3. While spaghetti is cooking,
heat oil in 10-inch (25 cm) noncorrosive skillet over medium-
high heat. Add garlic; cook
just until garlic begins to color,
45 to 60 seconds. Stir in
tomatoes, parsley, capers, basil, oregano, salt and the pepper flakes.

4. Add olives and anchovies
to skillet; cook over medium-
high heat, stirring constantly,
until most of the visible liquid
has evaporated and sauce is
slightly thickened, about 10
minutes. Pour sauce over
spaghetti in heated serving
bowl. Toss lightly and serve
immediately.

Makes 3 to 4 servings.

Fettuccine Alfredo

¾ pound (340 g) uncooked fettuccine

Boiling salted water

6 tablespoons (90 mL) unsalted butter

⅔ cup (160 mL) whipping cream

½ teaspoon (2 mL) salt

Large pinch ground white pepper

Large pinch ground nutmeg

1 cup (250 mL) freshly grated Parmesan cheese (about 3 ounces or 85 g)

2 tablespoons (30 mL) chopped fresh parsley

1. Cook fettuccine in large pot of boiling salted water just until al dente, 6 to 8 minutes; drain well. Return to dry pot.

2. While fettuccine is cooking, place butter and cream in 10-inch (25 cm) heavy skillet over medium-low heat. Cook, stir-ring constantly, until blended and mixture bubbles for 2 minutes. Stir in salt, pepper and nutmeg. Remove from heat. Gradually stir in Parmesan cheese until thoroughly blended and fairly smooth. Return skillet briefly to heat if necessary to completely blend cheese, but don't let sauce bubble or cheese will become lumpy and tough.

3. Pour sauce over fettuccine in pot. Place over low heat. Stir and toss with 2 forks until sauce is slightly thickened and fettuccine evenly coated, 2 to 3 minutes. Sprinkle with parsley. Serve immediately.

Makes 4 servings.

Fettuccine Carbonara

4 ounces (115 g) pancetta (Italian bacon) or lean American bacon, cut into ½-inch-(1.5 cm) wide strips

3 cloves garlic, cut into halves

¼ cup (60 mL) dry white wine

⅓ cup (80 mL) whipping cream

½ pound (225 g) uncooked fettuccine or spaghetti

Boiling salted water

1 large egg

1 large egg yolk

⅔ cup (160 mL) freshly grated Parmesan cheese (about 2 ounces or 60 g)

Large pinch ground white pepper

1. Cook and stir pancetta and garlic in 10-inch (25 cm) non-corrosive skillet over medium-low heat until pancetta is light brown, about 4 minutes. Discard garlic and all but 2 tablespoons (30 mL) of the drippings.

2. Add wine to skillet; cook over medium heat until wine is almost completely evaporated, about 3 minutes. Stir in cream; cook and stir 2 minutes. Remove from heat.

3. Cook fettuccine in large saucepan of boiling salted water just until al dente, 6 to 8 minutes; drain well. Return to dry saucepan.

4. Whisk egg and egg yolk in small bowl; whisk in ⅓ cup (80 mL) of the cheese and the pepper. Pour bacon-cream mixture over fettuccine in saucepan; toss to coat. Heat over medium-low heat just until hot. Stir in egg-cheese mixture. Toss to coat evenly. Immediately remove from heat. Serve with remaining cheese.

Makes 4 servings.

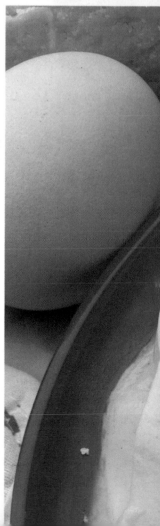

Spaghetti with Eggplant Sauce

1 small eggplant (about ¾
  pound or 340 g)
2 teaspoons (10 mL) salt
1 can (28 ounces or 790 g)
  Italian plum tomatoes
7 Italian- or Greek-style
  black olives
6 flat anchovy fillets
2 teaspoons (10 mL) drained
  capers
1 large green bell pepper
1 medium onion
2 medium cloves garlic
⅓ cup (80 mL) olive oil
2 teaspoons (10 mL) chopped
  fresh basil or ¾ teaspoon
  (4 mL) dried basil,
  crumbled
⅛ teaspoon (0.5 mL) hot red
  pepper sauce
¼ cup (60 mL) chopped fresh
  parsley
1 pound (450 g) uncooked
  spaghetti
Boiling salted water
Grated Parmesan or Romano
  cheese, if desired

1. Pare eggplant; cut into ¾-inch (2 cm) cubes. Place eggplant cubes in colander; sprinkle with the salt and toss. Let stand and drain in sink or over bowl, tossing occasionally, 1 hour.

2. Meanwhile, chop undrained tomatoes in can with scissors or knife; reserve. Pit olives. Rinse anchovies; pat dry. Chop olives, anchovies and capers together; reserve.

3. Rinse eggplant and drain well; squeeze dry in clean kitchen towel. Core, seed and chop green pepper. Chop onion; mince garlic.

4. Heat oil in 3-quart (3 L) non-corrosive saucepan over medium-high heat. Add eggplant, green pepper and onion; sauté 5 minutes. Add garlic; cook 30 seconds. Stir in reserved tomatoes and their liquid, the basil and red pepper sauce. Heat to boiling; reduce heat. Simmer covered 20 minutes. Uncover and cook, stirring occasionally, until sauce is thickened to coating consistency, about 10 minutes longer. Stir in reserved olive mixture and the parsley. Simmer covered 5 minutes longer.

5. Just before serving, cook spaghetti in large pot of boiling salted water just until al dente, 8 to 12 minutes; drain well. Toss spaghetti with sauce in heated serving bowl. Serve with cheese to sprinkle.

Makes 4 to 6 servings.

Spaghetti with Seafood Sauce

¼ cup (60 mL) cold water
1 tablespoon (15 mL) cornstarch
2 small green onions
2 medium cloves garlic
8 small fresh oysters
¼ pound (115 g) fresh scallops*
1 pound (450 g) fresh medium shrimp in shells
¼ cup (60 mL) butter
10 ounces (285 g) uncooked spaghetti
Boiling salted water
½ cup (125 mL) dry white wine
1¼ cups (310 mL) whipping cream
2 teaspoons (10 mL) fresh lemon juice
½ teaspoon (2 mL) salt
⅛ teaspoon (0.5 mL) pepper
2 tablespoons (30 mL) chopped fresh parsley
Lemon wedges

Note: *Occasionally, in some coastal areas, fresh scallops are available with the roe or coral attached. These are the or-

angish-pink-colored, crescent-shaped pieces shown in the photo, above right. If coral is present, separate it from the scallops and cook along with scallops in recipe.

1. Mix ¼ cup (60 mL) cold water and the cornstarch in cup until smooth; reserve. Trim and slice green onions. Mince garlic. Reserve.

2. Scrub oysters thoroughly with stiff brush under cold running water. Shuck oysters over bowl to catch liquor; reserve shells for garnish, if desired. Strain oyster liquor through triple thickness of dampened cheesecloth; reserve.

3. Rinse scallops under cold running water; drain and pat dry. Cut scallops into 1-inch (2.5 cm) pieces.

4. Shell shrimp under cold running water. Cut a shallow slit down the back of shrimp; pull out and discard intestinal vein. Pat shrimp dry.

5. Heat butter in large noncorrosive skillet over medium heat. When foam subsides, add oysters; sauté just until edges begin to curl, 1 to 2 minutes. Remove oysters with slotted spoon to plate. Add scallops and shrimp to pan; sauté just until opaque, 2 to 3 minutes. Remove scallops and shrimp with slotted spoon to separate plate. Reserve drippings in pan.

6. Cook spaghetti in large kettle of boiling salted water just until al dente, 8 to 12 minutes; drain well.

7. While spaghetti is cooking, sauté reserved garlic in drippings remaining in skillet over medium heat 30 seconds. Stir in wine; then stir in reserved oyster liquor and the cream. Heat to boiling. Cook over medium heat, stirring and scraping brown bits from bottom of pan, 5 minutes. Stir in reserved cornstarch mixture; simmer over low heat, stirring constantly, 3 minutes. Stir in lemon juice, salt and pepper. Stir in shrimp and scallops; cook just until heated through. Pour sauce over spaghetti in heated serving bowl. Top with reserved green onions, the parsley and oysters; toss. Garnish with reserved shells, if desired. Serve with lemon wedges.

Makes 3 to 4 servings.

Pesto

¼ cup (60 mL) plus 1 tablespoon (15 mL) olive oil
2 tablespoons (30 mL) pine nuts (pignolias)
1 cup (250 mL) tightly packed, rinsed, drained, stemmed fresh basil leaves (do not use dried basil)
2 medium cloves garlic
¼ teaspoon (1 mL) salt
¼ cup (60 mL) freshly grated Parmesan cheese
1½ tablespoons (22 mL) freshly grated Romano cheese

Serving Suggestions: Toss pesto with hot cooked buttered fettuccine or linguine; this recipe will dress ½ to ¾ pound (225 to 340 g) pasta. Stir small amount of pesto into broth-based vegetable or meat soups. Whisk small amount of pesto into vinaigrette for tossed salads. Mix pesto with softened butter to be used on steamed vegetables, poached fish or omelets.

1. Heat 1 tablespoon (15 mL) of the oil in small saucepan or skillet over medium-low heat. Add pine nuts; sauté, stirring

and shaking pan constantly until nuts are light brown, 30 to 45 seconds. Transfer nuts immediately to paper towel-lined plate to drain.

2. Combine pine nuts, basil leaves, garlic, salt and remaining ¼ cup (60 mL) oil in food processor or blender container. Process until mixture is evenly blended and pieces are very finely chopped.

3. Transfer basil mixture to small bowl. Stir in Parmesan and Romano cheeses. Pesto can be refrigerated, covered with thin layer of olive oil, up to 1 week; or pesto can be frozen for several months. Thaw and bring to room temperature before using.

Makes about ¾ cup (180 mL) pesto.

Sicilian Spaghetti

2 large eggplants (about 1½ pounds or 675 g each)
4 teaspoons (20 mL) salt
½ pound (225 g) uncooked spaghetti
Boiling salted water
1 large onion
2 medium cloves garlic
1 pound (450 g) ground beef chuck
2 tablespoons (30 mL) butter
1 can (14½ ounces or 415 g) whole peeled tomatoes
2 tablespoons (30 mL) tomato paste
¾ teaspoon (4 mL) dried oregano, crumbled
⅛ teaspoon (0.5 mL) pepper
1 package (10 ounces or 285 g) frozen peas, thawed
1 cup (250 mL) grated Parmesan cheese (about 3 ounces or 85 g)
1 cup (250 mL) shredded Cheddar cheese (about 3 ounces or 85 g)
¾ cup (180 mL) olive oil
½ cup (125 mL) fine dry unseasoned breadcrumbs
2 tablespoons (30 mL) chopped fresh parsley

1. Rinse eggplants; cut crosswise into ¼-inch (0.5 cm) thick slices. Sprinkle eggplant with 3 teaspoons (15 mL) of the salt; stand slices in colander. Let drain in sink 1 hour.

2. Meanwhile, cook spaghetti in large kettle of boiling salted water just until al dente, about 8 minutes. Drain well; place in large bowl.

3. Chop onion; mince garlic.

Cook beef in 1 tablespoon (15 mL) of the butter in 10-inch (25 cm) noncorrosive skillet over medium-high heat, breaking up beef into fine pieces, until brown, 8 to 10 minutes. Add onion and garlic to skillet; cook and stir over medium heat 5 minutes. Add liquid from tomatoes. Chop tomatoes fine; add to skillet. Stir in tomato paste, oregano, remaining 1 teaspoon (5 mL) salt and the pepper. Heat to boiling; reduce heat to medium-low. Cook uncovered until liquid is reduced by half, 15 to 20 minutes. Add meat sauce and peas to spaghetti; toss with 2 forks. Add cheeses; toss well.

4. Rinse eggplant; drain well. Press slices dry with paper toweling. Heat 1½ tablespoons (22 mL) of the oil in 12-inch (30 cm) skillet over medium-high heat; add as many eggplant slices as will fit in single layer. Cook, turning slices over once, until light brown, 1 to 2 minutes per side; remove to paper towel-lined wire rack. Repeat, frying remaining eggplant in remaining oil in batches.

5. Heat oven to 350°F (180°C). Spread remaining 1 tablespoon (15 mL) butter on bottom and sides of 9-inch (23 cm) springform pan; coat with half the breadcrumbs. Starting at center and working out to edges, cover bottom of pan with a layer of overlapping eggplant slices. Cover side of pan with overlapping eggplant slices; spoon some of the spaghetti mixture into pan and use to support side slices as you work. Add remaining spaghetti mixture to pan and pack down; cover with overlapping eggplant slices. Sprinkle with remaining breadcrumbs.

6. Bake until top is golden brown, about 35 minutes. Cool in pan on wire rack 5 minutes. Remove sides of pan. Sprinkle top with parsley. Cut into wedges to serve.

Makes 6 to 8 servings.

Cannelloni

Tomato Sauce (recipe follows)
White Sauce (recipe follows)
2 tablespoons (30 mL) butter
1 pound (450 g) boneless skinless chicken breasts
1 medium onion, chopped
1 clove garlic, minced
2 tablespoons (30 mL) dry white wine
1 large egg
2 teaspoons (10 mL) tomato paste
½ teaspoon (2 mL) salt
½ teaspoon (2 mL) dried rosemary, crumbled
⅛ teaspoon (0.5 mL) pepper
⅛ teaspoon (0.5 mL) nutmeg
1 package (10 ounces or 285 g) frozen spinach, thawed and squeezed dry
10 uncooked cannelloni shells
Boiling salted water
1 cup (250 mL) shredded mozzarella cheese
¼ cup (60 mL) grated Parmesan cheese

1. Prepare Tomato Sauce. Prepare White Sauce.

2. Heat butter in medium skillet over medium heat. Add chicken; cook until brown, 5 to 6 minutes per side. Remove chicken to plate; let cool.

3. Add onion and garlic to drippings in skillet; sauté over medium heat until onion is soft, about 5 minutes. Add wine; cook and stir until wine is evaporated, about 1 minute. Transfer onion mixture to medium bowl. Whisk in egg, tomato paste, salt, rosemary, pepper, nutmeg and ⅓ cup (80 mL) of the White Sauce. Finely chop chicken and spinach; stir into onion mixture.

4. Heat oven to 350°F (180°C). Cook cannelloni shells in large pot of boiling salted water just until al dente, 6 to 10 minutes. Drain shells; rinse under cold water to stop the cooking. Drain well.

5. Coat bottom of 13 × 9 × 2-inch (33 × 23 × 5 cm) baking pan with ¼ cup (60 mL) of the Tomato Sauce. Fill each cannelloni shell with about ¼ cup (60 mL) chicken mixture; place in baking pan. Spoon remaining White Sauce evenly over cannelloni; top with remaining Tomato Sauce. Sprinkle with cheeses. Bake until top is golden, about 35 minutes.

Makes 4 to 5 servings.

Tomato Sauce

1 large onion, chopped
1 medium clove garlic, minced
1 tablespoon (15 mL) olive oil
1 can (16 ounces or 450 g) whole peeled tomatoes
2 tablespoons (30 mL) tomato paste
¼ teaspoon (1 mL) salt
¼ teaspoon (1 mL) dried thyme, crumbled
¼ teaspoon (1 mL) dried rosemary, crumbled
⅛ teaspoon (0.5 mL) pepper

1. Sauté onion and garlic in oil in medium noncorrosive saucepan over medium heat until onion is soft, about 5 minutes. Remove from heat.

2. Press tomatoes and their liquid through sieve into saucepan; discard seeds. Stir remaining ingredients into sauce. Heat to boiling; reduce heat to medium-low. Cook uncovered, stirring occasionally, 10 minutes. Remove from heat and reserve.

White Sauce

3 tablespoons (45 mL) butter
3 tablespoons (45 mL) all-purpose flour
½ teaspoon (2 mL) salt
1¾ cups (430 mL) half-and-half

1. Melt butter in small saucepan over medium heat. Stir in flour and salt; cook and stir until bubbly.

2. Whisk half-and-half into saucepan; cook and stir until sauce thickens and bubbles for 1 minute. Remove from heat; reserve covered.

Summer Spaghetti

1 pound (450 g) firm, ripe fresh plum tomatoes
1 medium onion
6 pitted green olives
2 medium cloves garlic
⅓ cup (80 mL) chopped fresh parsley
2 tablespoons (30 mL) finely shredded fresh basil or ¾ teaspoon (4 mL) dried basil, crumbled
2 teaspoons (10 mL) drained capers
½ teaspoon (2 mL) paprika
¼ teaspoon (1 mL) dried oregano, crumbled
1 tablespoon (15 mL) red wine vinegar
½ cup (125 mL) olive oil
1 pound (450 g) uncooked spaghetti
Boiling salted water

1. Chop tomatoes coarsely. Chop onion and olives. Mince garlic. Combine tomatoes, onion, olives, garlic, parsley,

basil, capers, paprika and oregano in medium bowl; toss well. Drizzle vinegar over tomato mixture. Then pour oil over tomato mixture. Stir until thoroughly mixed. Refrigerate covered at least 6 hours or overnight.

2. Just before serving, cook spaghetti in large kettle of boiling salted water just until al dente, 8 to 12 minutes; drain well. Immediately toss hot pasta with cold marinated tomato sauce. Serve at once.

Makes 4 to 6 servings.

Note: In this dish, the contact of the very cold sauce with the hot spaghetti releases a unique and delicious flavor. The resulting tepid pasta salad makes a refreshing lunch or light supper for a hot summer day. Or, you may serve the versatile sauce as a relish with grilled meats, as a dressing for mixed greens, or stirred into cooled cooked rice.

Pasta with Oil & Garlic

½ pound (225 g) uncooked pasta such as plain or spinach fettuccine, spaghetti or linguine
Boiling salted water
⅓ cup (80 mL) olive oil
3 medium cloves garlic, minced
¼ cup (60 mL) chopped fresh parsley
½ teaspoon (2 mL) salt
⅛ teaspoon (0.5 mL) pepper
½ cup (125 mL) freshly grated Parmesan cheese (about 1½ ounces or 45 g)

1. Cook pasta in large kettle of boiling salted water just until al dente, 6 to 12 minutes; drain well. Keep warm.

2. Heat oil in 10-inch (25 cm) skillet over low heat. Add garlic to skillet; cook gently until light gold, 2 to 3 minutes. Do not brown garlic or it will become bitter. Remove pan from heat. Stir in parsley, salt and pepper.

3. Add hot pasta to skillet. Toss to coat evenly. Serve immediately with cheese to sprinkle.

Makes 3 to 4 servings.

Spinach Lasagne

1 can (28 ounces or 790 g)
   Italian plum tomatoes
1 pound (450 g) ground beef
   chuck
1 tablespoon (15 mL) olive
   oil
¼ pound (115 g) fresh
   mushrooms, thinly sliced
1 medium onion, chopped
1 medium clove garlic,
   minced
1¼ teaspoons (6 mL) salt
¾ teaspoon (4 mL) dried
   oregano, crumbled
¾ teaspoon (4 mL) dried
   basil, crumbled
¼ teaspoon (1 mL) pepper
9 uncooked lasagne noodles
Boiling salted water
¼ cup (60 mL) plus 1
   tablespoon (15 mL) butter
¼ cup (60 mL) all-purpose
   flour
⅛ teaspoon (0.5 mL) ground
   nutmeg
2 cups (500 mL) milk
1½ cups (375 mL) shredded
   mozzarella cheese
½ cup (125 mL) grated
   Parmesan cheese
1 package (10 ounces or
   285 g) frozen chopped
   spinach, thawed and
   squeezed dry

1. For meat sauce: Press tomatoes and their liquid through sieve into bowl; discard seeds. Cook beef in oil in 10-inch (25 cm) noncorrosive skillet over medium-high heat, breaking up beef into fine pieces, until brown, 8 to 10 minutes. Stir in mushrooms, onion and garlic; cook over medium heat until onion is soft, about 5 minutes. Stir in tomatoes, ¾ teaspoon (4 mL) of the salt, the oregano, basil and ⅛ teaspoon (0.5 mL) of the pepper. Heat to boiling; reduce heat to low. Simmer covered, stirring occasionally, 40 minutes. Uncover and simmer until sauce is thick, 15 to 20 minutes longer. Reserve.

2. Add lasagne noodles to large pot of boiling salted water 1 at a time, allowing noodles to soften and fit into pan. Cook, stirring gently occasionally, just until noodles are al dente, about 10 minutes. Drain noodles; place in large bowl of cold water to stop the cooking. Change water once. Let noodles stand in water.

3. For cheese sauce: Melt ¼ cup (60 mL) of the butter in medium saucepan over medium heat. Stir in flour, remaining ½ teaspoon (2 mL) salt, remaining ⅛ teaspoon (0.5 mL) pepper and the nutmeg; cook and stir until bubbly. Whisk in milk; cook, stirring constantly, until sauce thickens and bubbles for 1 minute. Remove from heat. Stir in 1 cup (250 mL) of the mozzarella cheese and ¼ cup (60 mL) of the Parmesan cheese. Stir until smooth. Reserve.

4. Heat oven to 350°F (180°C). Spread remaining 1 tablespoon (15 mL) butter on bottom and sides of 12 × 8 × 2-inch (30 × 20 × 5 cm) baking dish. Drain noodles; spread in

single layer on clean kitchen (not paper) towel. Pat noodles dry.

5. Arrange 3 of the lasagne noodles in single layer, overlapping slightly, in bottom of baking dish. Top with half the reserved meat sauce; spread even. Spread half the reserved cheese sauce over meat sauce in even layer. Repeat layers once, using 3 more noodles, the remaining meat sauce and the remaining cheese sauce. Crumble spinach and sprinkle loosely over cheese sauce in even layer; pat down lightly. Arrange remaining 3 lasagne noodles in layer over spinach.

6. Mix remaining ½ cup (125 mL) mozzarella cheese and remaining ¼ cup (60 mL) Parmesan cheese in a cup. Sprinkle mixed cheeses evenly on top of lasagne. Bake until top is golden and edges are bubbly, about 40 minutes. Let lasagne

stand 10 minutes before serving.

Makes 6 servings.

Spaghetti Bolognese

2 tablespoons (30 mL) olive oil
1 medium onion, chopped
1 pound (450 g) ground beef chuck
½ small carrot, pared and finely chopped
½ stalk celery, finely chopped
1 cup (250 mL) dry white wine
½ cup (125 mL) milk
⅛ teaspoon (0.5 mL) ground nutmeg
1 can (14½ ounces or 415 g) whole peeled tomatoes
1 cup (250 mL) beef broth
3 tablespoons (45 mL) tomato paste
1 teaspoon (5 mL) each salt and dried basil, crumbled
½ teaspoon (2 mL) dried thyme, crumbled
⅛ teaspoon (0.5 mL) pepper
1 bay leaf
1 pound (450 g) uncooked spaghetti
Boiling salted water
1 cup (250 mL) freshly grated Parmesan cheese (about 3 ounces or 85 g)

1. Heat oil in 12-inch (30 cm) noncorrosive skillet over medium heat. Add onion;

sauté until soft, 4 to 5 minutes. Add beef to skillet. Cook, breaking up meat into fine pieces, until meat loses its raw color, about 6 minutes; do not brown meat.

2. Stir carrot and celery into meat mixture; cook over medium-high heat 2 minutes. Stir in wine; cook until wine is evaporated, 4 to 6 minutes. Stir in milk and nutmeg; reduce heat to medium and cook until milk is evaporated, 3 to 4 minutes. Remove from heat.

3. Press tomatoes and their

liquid through sieve into bowl; discard seeds. Stir sieved tomatoes, beef broth, tomato paste, salt, basil, thyme, pepper and bay leaf into meat mixture. Heat to boiling; reduce heat to low. Simmer uncovered, stirring frequently, until most of the liquid has evaporated and sauce is thick, 1 to 1½ hours. Remove and discard bay leaf.

4. Just before serving tir cook spaghetti in large kettle boiling salted water just u al dente, 8 to 12 minutes; dr well. Ladle meat sauce o spaghetti in heated bo Sprinkle cheese on top.

Makes 4 to 6 servings.

Spaghetti with Piccantes Chillies Sauce

4 green onions
½ medium red bell pepper
2 medium or 3 small cloves garlic
2 or 3 small red or green hot chili peppers
½ pound (225 g) uncooked spaghetti
Boiling salted water
6 tablespoons (90 mL) butter
½ cup (125 mL) freshly grated Parmesan cheese (about 1½ ounces or 45 g)
3 tablespoons (45 mL) minced fresh parsley
½ teaspoon (2 mL) salt
⅛ teaspoon (0.5 mL) pepper

1. Trim green onions; slice thinly. Core, seed and mince bell pepper. Crush garlic through a press or mince. Seed and mince chili peppers. (*Caution:* Chili peppers can sting and irritate skin; wear rubber gloves when handling peppers and do not touch eyes.)

2. Cook spaghetti in large pot of boiling salted water just until al dente, 8 to 12 minutes; drain well.

3. While spaghetti is cooking, heat butter in 10-inch (25 cm) skillet over medium-high heat. When foam subsides, add green onions, bell pepper, garlic and chili peppers. Cook, stirring constantly, until onions are soft, about 2 minutes. Remove from heat.

4. Quickly add hot spaghe to skillet; toss well. Ac cheese, parsley, salt and pe per; toss. Serve immediately.

Makes 3 to 4 servings.

Ravioli

Sauce

1 can (28 ounces or 790 g) Italian plum tomatoes
1 large clove garlic, minced
⅓ cup (80 mL) butter
1 can (8 ounces or 225 g) tomato sauce
¾ teaspoon (4 mL) salt
½ teaspoon (2 mL) each ground allspice, dried basil, crumbled, and dried rosemary, crumbled
⅛ teaspoon (0.5 mL) pepper

Filling

5 ounces (140 g) fresh spinach, cleaned, cooked and squeezed very dry
1 small chicken breast, cooked, skinned, boned
3 ounces (85 g) cooked ham
1½ ounces (45 g) hard salami
1 medium clove garlic
6 ounces (170 g) ground beef
½ cup (125 mL) chopped fresh parsley
2 large eggs
¼ teaspoon (1 mL) each ground allspice and salt

Dough

4 cups (1 L) all-purpose flour
¼ teaspoon (1 mL) salt
2 large eggs
1 tablespoon (15 mL) olive oil
⅔ to 1 cup (160 to 250 mL) water

1 large egg yolk
1 teaspoon (5 mL) milk
Boiling salted water

1. For sauce: Press tomatoes and their liquid through sieve into bowl; discard seeds. Sauté garlic in butter in large noncorrosive saucepan over medium heat 30 seconds. Stir in tomatoes and remaining sauce ingredients. Simmer covered 30 minutes. Uncover pan; simmer, stirring occasionally, until thickened to coating consistency, about 15 minutes longer. Reserve.

2. For filling: Mince spinach, chicken, ham, salami and garlic; combine in medium bowl with remaining filling ingredients. Mix well. Refrigerate.

3. For dough: Mix flour and salt in large bowl. Whisk eggs, oil and ⅔ cup (160 mL) of the water in small bowl; gradually stir into flour mixture with fork. Add as much of the remaining water as needed to form firm but pliable dough. Knead on floured surface 5 minutes. Let rest wrapped in plastic 30 minutes.

4. Divide dough into 4 pieces. Roll, cut and fill 1 piece at a time; keep unused pieces wrapped. Roll out dough on lightly floured surface to 1/16-inch (2 mm) or less thick. Cut dough into 4-inch-(10 cm) wide strips. Place teaspoonfuls (5 mL) of filling along one long edge of each strip at 2-inch (5 cm) intervals. Brush dough on

long edge and between filling with egg yolk mixed with the milk. Fold dough over filling; press firmly between filling and along long edge to seal. Cut ravioli apart with fluted pastry wheel.

5. Cook a quarter of the ravioli at a time in large pot of boiling salted water just until al dente, 3 to 5 minutes. Remove with slotted spoon draining well; add to reserved sauce. When all ravioli have been cooked, heat in sauce to boiling; reduce heat to medium-low. Simmer uncovered 6 to 8 minutes. Serve at once.

Makes 6 servings.

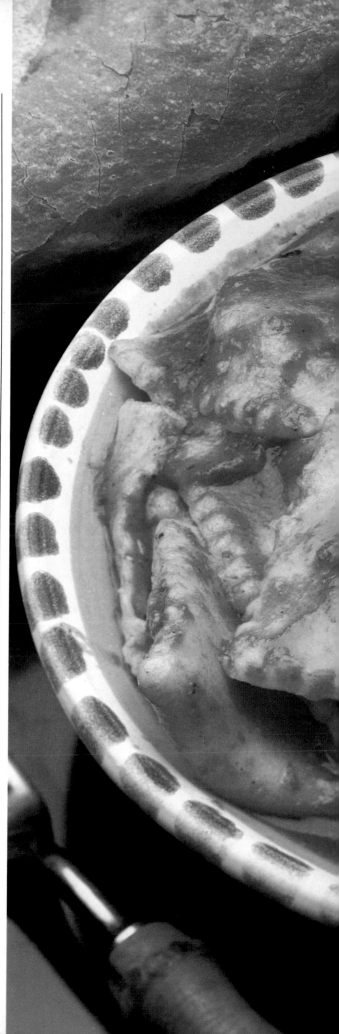

Spaghetti Marinara

8 fresh oysters
½ pound (225 g) fresh
  scallops (see note for
  Seafood Sauce, page 28)
6 flat anchovy fillets
⅓ cup (80 mL) chopped
  onion
2 tablespoons (30 mL) olive
  oil
1 large clove garlic, minced
½ cup (125 mL) dry white
  wine
10 ounces (285 g) uncooked
  spaghetti
Boiling salted water
5 large ripe fresh tomatoes,
  seeded and chopped
1 tablespoon (15 mL) tomato
  paste
¾ teaspoon (4 mL) dried
  basil, crumbled
¾ teaspoon (4 mL) salt
½ teaspoon (2 mL) dried
  oregano, crumbled
⅛ teaspoon (0.5 mL) pepper
1 pound (450 g) fresh
  medium shrimp, shelled
  and deveined
3 tablespoons (45 mL)
  chopped fresh parsley

1. Scrub oysters; shuck over bowl; discard shells. Strain oyster liquor; reserve. Cut scallops into ¾-inch (2 cm) pieces. Drain and mince anchovies.

2. Sauté onion in oil in 3-quart (3 L) noncorrosive saucepan over medium-high heat until soft, about 4 minutes. Add garlic; cook 30 seconds. Add wine; cook until wine is completely evaporated, 4 to 5 minutes. Remove from heat.

3. Cook spaghetti in large kettle of boiling salted water just until al dente, 8 to 12 minutes; drain well.

4. While spaghetti is cooking, stir tomatoes, oyster liquor, anchovies, tomato paste, basil, salt, oregano and pepper into onion mixture. Heat to boiling; reduce heat to medium. Cook uncovered, stirring occasionally, until sauce is very thick, about 20 minutes. Stir in shrimp, scallops and oysters. Cook covered, stirring occasionally, just until shrimp are cooked through, 2 to 3 minutes. Stir in parsley. Toss sauce with spaghetti; serve immediately

Makes 3 to 4 servings.

Tomato Sauces

Neapolitan Sauce

1 can (28 ounces or 790 g)
  Italian plum tomatoes
2 tablespoons (30 mL) butter
1 tablespoon (15 mL) olive
  oil
1 teaspoon (5 mL) dried
  basil, crumbled
½ teaspoon (2 mL) salt
⅛ teaspoon (0.5 mL) pepper

3 tablespoons (45 mL)
  chopped fresh parsley
½ pound (225 g) spaghetti,
  cooked
½ cup (125 mL) freshly
  grated Parmesan cheese,
  if desired

1. Press tomatoes and their liquid through sieve into bowl; discard seeds.

2. Heat butter and oil in 2-quart (2 L) noncorrosive sauce-

pan over medium heat. Stir in sieved tomatoes, basil, salt and pepper. Heat to boiling; reduce heat to medium-low. Cook uncovered, stirring frequently, until sauce is reduced and measures 2 cups (500 mL), 30 to 40 minutes. Stir in parsley. Toss with spaghetti. Serve immediately with Parmesan cheese to sprinkle.

Makes 2 to 3 servings.

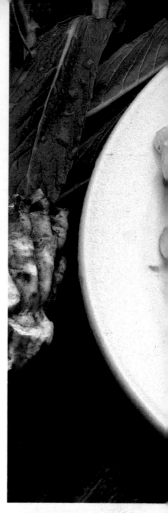

Pizzaiola Sauce

1 can (28 ounces or 790 g)
  Italian plum tomatoes
2 cloves garlic
1 tablespoon (15 mL) olive
  oil
¾ teaspoon (4 mL) dried
  marjoram, crumbled
½ teaspoon (2 mL) salt
⅛ teaspoon (0.5 mL) pepper
2 tablespoons (30 mL)
  minced fresh parsley

½ pound (225 g) spaghetti,
  cooked
½ cup (125 mL) freshly
  grated Parmesan cheese,
  if desired

1. Press tomatoes and their liquid through sieve into bowl; discard seeds. Cut garlic in half.

2. Heat oil in 2-quart (2 L) noncorrosive saucepan over medium heat. Add garlic; cook and stir until garlic is golden

but not brown, 2 to 3 minutes. Remove and discard garlic. Add sieved tomatoes to oil; stir in marjoram, salt and pepper. Heat to boiling; reduce heat to medium-low. Cook uncovered, stirring frequently, until sauce is reduced and measures 2 cups (500 mL), 30 to 40 minutes. Stir in parsley. Toss with spaghetti. Serve immediately with Parmesan cheese to sprinkle.

Makes 2 to 3 servings.

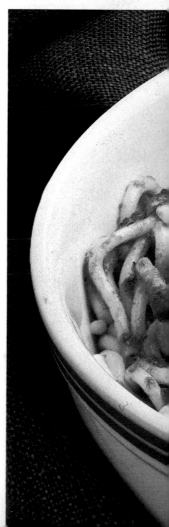

Gnocchi, Polenta & Rice

Gnocchi Verdi

2 packages (10 ounces or 285 g each) frozen spinach
1 cup (250 mL) ricotta cheese
2 large eggs
⅔ cup (160 mL) freshly grated Parmesan cheese (about 2 ounces or 60 g)
1 cup (250 mL) plus 3 tablespoons (45 mL) all-purpose flour
½ teaspoon (2 mL) salt
⅛ teaspoon (0.5 mL) pepper
⅛ teaspoon (0.5 mL) ground nutmeg
Boiling salted water
3 tablespoons (45 mL) butter

1. Cook spinach according to package directions. Drain well; let cool. Squeeze spinach very dry. Chop spinach very fine; place in medium bowl. Stir in ricotta cheese. Add eggs; mix well. Add ⅓ cup (80 mL) of the Parmesan cheese, 3 tablespoons (45 mL) of the flour, the salt, pepper and nutmeg; stir to mix very well. Refrigerate covered 1 hour.

2. Spread remaining 1 cup (250 mL) flour in shallow baking pan. Press a heaping table-

spoonful of spinach mixture between spoon and hand to form oval gnocchi; place on flour. Repeat until all spinach mixture is used.

3. Roll gnocchi lightly in flour to coat evenly; discard excess flour. Slip 8 to 12 gnocchi into large kettle of boiling salted water; reduce heat to medium. Cook uncovered until gnocchi are slightly puffed and medium-firm to the touch, about 5 minutes. Remove gnocchi with slotted spoon to paper towel-lined plate; then transfer immediately to greased flameproof shallow baking dish. Reheat water to

boiling. Continue cooking and draining gnocchi in batches until all have been cooked. Arrange gnocchi so that they are in single layer in baking dish.

4. Heat broiler. Melt butter in small saucepan. Spoon butter over gnocchi; sprinkle with remaining ⅓ cup (80 mL) Parmesan cheese. Broil gnocchi, 5 inches (13 cm) from heat source, until cheese topping is light brown, 2 to 3 minutes. Serve at once.

Makes about 24 gnocchi; 4 to 6 servings.

Gnocchi alla Romana

Vegetable oil
3 cups (750 mL) milk
1½ teaspoons (7 mL) salt
Large pinch ground nutmeg
Large pinch pepper
1 cup (250 mL) plus 2
   tablespoons (30 mL)
   semolina
2 large egg yolks, lightly
   beaten
1 cup (250 mL) freshly grated
   Parmesan cheese (about 3
   ounces or 85 g)
6 tablespoons (90 mL) butter

1. Line bottom of 15½ × 10½ × 1-inch (39 × 26.5 × 2.5 cm) baking pan with aluminum foil. Generously oil the foil.

2. Heat milk, salt, nutmeg and pepper in heavy 3-quart (3 L) saucepan over medium-high heat just to simmering. Do not boil; reduce heat to medium-low. Begin whisking or stirring milk briskly and add semolina in thin steady stream, taking care not to let lumps form. Cook, stirring frequently, until thick enough for spoon to stand upright and unsupported in center of mixture, 5 to 10 minutes. Reduce heat to low; continue cooking, stirring constantly, until very thick, about 5 minutes longer. Remove from heat.

3. Add egg yolks, ¾ cup (180 mL) of the cheese and 2 tablespoons (30 mL) of the butter to semolina mixture; stir until butter is melted and mixture is smooth.

4. Transfer mixture to prepared pan. Pat out with spatula to ⅜-inch (1 cm) thickness. Refrigerate uncovered until cold, at least 1 hour.

5. Heat oven to 425°F (220°C). Turn mixture out of pan onto flat surface; peel off foil. Cut

gnocchi out of mixture with 2-inch (5 cm) round cutter. Arrange gnocchi overlapping in 10-inch (25 cm) shallow flameproof baking dish. Melt remaining 4 tablespoons (60 mL) butter in small saucepan. Drizzle melted butter over gnocchi; sprinkle with remaining ¼ cup (60 mL) cheese. Bake until tops of gnocchi are crisp and golden, 20 to 25 minutes. Place under broiler about 4 inches (10 cm) from heat, until light brown, 1 to 2 minutes. Serve at once.

Makes 4 to 6 servings.

Polenta

6 cups (1.5 L) water
2 teaspoons (10 mL) salt
2 cups (500 mL) yellow
   cornmeal
¼ cup (60 mL) plus 2
   teaspoons (10 mL)
   vegetable oil

Note: Polenta, an important component of Northern Italian cooking, is the basis of countless dishes. The basic preparation presented here can be served in two forms. Hot, freshly made polenta, prepared through step 1, can be mixed with ⅓ cup (80 mL) each butter and grated Parmesan cheese and served as a first course; or it can be poured onto a large platter and topped with Bolognese Sauce (see Index for recipe) or other hearty meat sauces. Fried polenta, prepared through step 4, is appropriate as an appetizer or as an accompaniment for roasted or sautéed meats such as Venetian Liver with Onions (see Index for recipe).

1. Heat 6 cups (1.5 L) water and the salt in heavy 4-quart (4 L) Dutch oven or saucepan to boiling. Begin whisking water vigorously and add cornmeal in very thin but

steady stream, taking care not to let lumps form. Reduce heat to low. Continue cooking **polenta** uncovered, stirring **frequently,** until very thick, 40 **to 60 minutes.** Polenta is ready **when thick enough** for spoon **to stand** upright and unsupported in center of mixture. Polenta can be served at this point (see Note at left).

2. For fried polenta, coat inside of 11 × 7 × 2-inch (28 × 18 × 5 cm) baking pan with 2 teaspoons (10 mL) of the oil.

Transfer polenta mixture to baking pan; spread in smooth, even layer. Let stand uncovered at room temperature until completely cooled and very firm, at least 6 hours.

3. Unmold polenta onto cutting board. Cut polenta crosswise into 1¼-inch- (3 cm) wide strips. Cut strips crosswise into 2- to 3-inch-(5 to 8 cm) long pieces.

4. Heat remaining ¼ cup (60 mL) oil in large heavy skillet over medium-high heat until hot; reduce heat to medium. Fry half the polenta pieces at a time, turning as needed, until golden on all sides, 4 to 5 minutes.

Makes 6 to 8 servings.

Vegetable Risotto

½ pound (225 g) eggplant (about 1 small)
1¾ teaspoons (9 mL) salt
1 small zucchini
1 small red bell pepper
1 small green bell pepper
¼ pound (115 g) fresh mushrooms
4 tablespoons (60 mL) butter
½ cup (125 mL) fresh or frozen peas
1 large onion
2 tablespoons (30 mL) olive oil
2 cups (500 mL) uncooked rice
2 cups (500 mL) chicken broth
1¾ cups (430 mL) hot water
⅛ teaspoon (0.5 mL) black pepper
⅔ cup (160 mL) grated Parmesan cheese (about 2 ounces or 60 g)

1. Cut eggplant crosswise into ½-inch- (1.5 cm) thick slices. Sprinkle both sides with 1 teaspoon (5 mL) of the salt. Let stand in colander in sink for 1 hour to drain.

2. Thinly slice zucchini. Core, seed and dice red and green bell peppers. Trim mushrooms; wipe clean with damp kitchen towel and thinly slice.

3. Heat 2 tablespoons (30 mL) of the butter in 4-quart (4 L) saucepan over medium-high heat. Add mushrooms; sauté 3 minutes. Transfer mushrooms to medium bowl. Rinse and drain eggplant; press dry between paper towels. Cut eggplant into ½-inch (1.5 cm) cubes. Add eggplant, zucchini, bell peppers and peas to mushrooms in bowl.

4. Chop onion. Heat remaining 2 tablespoons (30 mL) butter and the oil in the 4-quart (4 L) saucepan over medium heat. Add onion; sauté until onion is soft, about 5 minutes. Stir in rice; cook and stir 2 minutes.

5. Stir broth, 1¾ cups (430 mL) hot water, remaining ¾ teaspoon (4 mL) salt and the black pepper into rice mixture. Heat over high heat to boiling; reduce heat to low. Simmer covered, stirring occasionally, 8 minutes. Add vegetables; stir well. Cook uncovered, stirring

frequently, until rice is tender and all liquid is absorbed, about 10 minutes longer. Remove from heat; stir in cheese.

6. Pack rice mixture into greased 3-quart (3 L) bowl. Let stand 3 minutes. Cover bowl with serving plate; invert and lift off bowl. Serve risotto at once.

Makes 8 to 10 servings.

Rice & Peas

2 pounds (900 g) fresh peas in pods*
1 medium onion
1 stalk celery
2¼ to 3 cups (560 to 750 mL) chicken broth**
¼ cup (60 mL) butter
¾ cup (180 mL) uncooked rice
½ cup (125 mL) dry white wine
½ teaspoon (2 mL) salt
Large pinch pepper
¼ cup (60 mL) grated Parmesan cheese

Notes: *One package (10 ounces or 285 g) frozen peas, thawed, can be substituted for fresh, if desired; add to rice mixture in step 3 after rice has simmered for 6 minutes.

**This dish traditionally has the consistency of a thick soup and is eaten with a spoon; for this consistency, use the larger amount of broth. If you prefer thicker consistency, use the smaller amount of broth.

1. Shell peas; discard pods. Chop onion and celery. Heat broth in small saucepan over medium heat to simmering; keep hot over low heat.

2. Heat butter in 2½-quart (2.5 L) noncorrosive saucepan over medium heat. When foam subsides, add onion and celery; sauté until onion is soft, about 5 minutes. Stir in rice; cook and stir 2 minutes.

3. Stir hot broth into rice mixture in saucepan; stir in wine, salt and pepper. Add peas. Heat over high heat to boiling; reduce heat to low. Simmer covered, stirring occasionally, until rice is tender but firm to the bite, about 12 minutes. Remove from heat.

4. Stir cheese into cooked rice mixture. Serve at once.

Makes 6 servings.

Rice Croquettes

1 cup (250 mL) chicken broth
2 tablespoons (30 mL) butter
1 small onion, chopped
½ cup (125 mL) uncooked rice
¼ cup (60 mL) dry white wine
¼ teaspoon (1 mL) salt
Pinch pepper
Pinch saffron threads
¼ cup (60 mL) grated Parmesan cheese
1 large egg
1½ ounces (45 g) mozzarella cheese, cut into ½-inch (1.5 cm) cubes
Vegetable oil
½ cup (125 mL) fine dry unseasoned breadcrumbs

1. Heat broth in small saucepan over medium heat to simmering; keep hot over low heat.

2. Heat butter in heavy 1½-quart (1.5 L) saucepan over medium heat; when foam subsides add onion. Sauté until onion is soft, 3 to 4 minutes. Stir in rice; cook and stir 2 minutes.

3. Stir half the hot broth, the wine, salt and pepper into rice mixture; reduce heat to medium-low. Cook uncovered, stirring frequently, until liquid is absorbed, 5 to 8 minutes. Meanwhile, crush saffron in mortar with pestle to a powder; stir into remaining broth. Add saffron-flavored broth to rice mixture. Continue cooking uncovered, stirring frequently, until rice is tender and broth is absorbed, about 5 minutes longer. Remove from heat; stir in Parmesan cheese. Let stand at room temperature until completely cool, about 45 minutes.

4. Lightly beat egg in small bowl; stir into cooled rice mixture.

5. To form croquettes: Place scant tablespoonful (scant 15 mL) of rice mixture in palm of hand; top with 1 cheese cube. Cover cheese with second tablespoonful (15 mL) of rice; press between palms to form ball, making sure that cheese is completely covered with rice mixture. Place croquettes on waxed paper.

6. Heat 2 inches (5 cm) oil in medium saucepan to 350°F (180°C). Heat oven to 200°F (95°C). Spread breadcrumbs in shallow bowl. Roll croquettes in crumbs to coat evenly; press between palms. Transfer 3 or 4 croquettes with wire skimmer to oil; fry until brown, about 3 minutes. Remove croquettes with skimmer to paper towel-lined plate; place in oven. Repeat until all croquettes have been fried; leave in oven 5 minutes before serving to be sure cheese has melted.

Makes about 10 croquettes.

Risotto Milanese

3½ to 4 cups (875 mL to 1 L) chicken broth
7 tablespoons (105 mL) butter
1 large onion, chopped
1½ cups (375 mL) uncooked rice
½ cup (125 mL) dry white wine
½ teaspoon (2 mL) salt
Pinch pepper
¼ teaspoon (1 mL) saffron threads
¼ cup (60 mL) grated Parmesan cheese

1. Heat broth in small saucepan over medium heat to simmering; keep hot over low heat.

2. Heat 6 tablespoons (90 mL) of the butter in heavy 10-inch (25 cm) skillet or 2½-quart (2.5 L) saucepan over medium

heat. When foam subsides, add onion; sauté until onion is soft, about 5 minutes. Stir in rice; cook and stir 2 minutes. Stir in wine, salt and pepper. Cook uncovered over medium-high heat, stirring occasionally, until wine is evaporated, 3 to 5 minutes.

3. Measure ½ cup (125 mL) of the hot broth; stir into rice. Adjust heat during this step between medium and low to maintain simmer. Cook uncovered, stirring frequently, until broth is absorbed. Repeat this process of adding ½ cup

(125 mL) broth and cooking until absorbed until a total of 2 cups (500 mL) broth has been added. Meanwhile, crush saffron in mortar with pestle to a powder; stir in ½ cup (125 mL) of the remaining broth to dissolve saffron. Add saffron-flavored broth to rice and cook until absorbed. Continue adding remaining broth, ½ cup (125 mL) at a time, and cooking, until rice is tender but firm to the bite and mixture has slightly creamy consistency. Not all the broth may be required. Total cooking time will be about 20 minutes.

4. Remove risotto from heat. Stir in remaining 1 tablespoon (15 mL) butter and the cheese. Serve at once.

Makes 6 to 8 servings.

Note: Risotto Milanese is the traditional accompaniment to Osso Buco (see Index for recipe). It is also an appropriate first course for or accompaniment to roasted meat or poultry dishes.

Pizza

½ tablespoon (7 mL) active dry yeast
1 teaspoon (5 mL) sugar
½ cup (125 mL) very warm water (105°F to 115°F or 40°C to 46°C)
1¾ cups (430 mL) all-purpose flour
¾ teaspoon (4 mL) salt
2 tablespoons (30 mL) olive oil
1 can (14½ ounces or 415 g) whole peeled tomatoes
1 medium onion
1 medium clove garlic
2 tablespoons (30 mL) tomato paste
1 teaspoon (5 mL) dried oregano, crumbled
½ teaspoon (2 mL) dried basil, crumbled
⅛ teaspoon (0.5 mL) black pepper
½ small red bell pepper
½ small green bell pepper
⅓ cup (80 mL) pitted ripe olives
4 fresh medium mushrooms
1 can (2 ounces or 60 g) flat anchovy fillets
1¾ cups (430 mL) shredded mozzarella cheese
½ cup (125 mL) grated Parmesan cheese

1. Sprinkle yeast and ½ teaspoon (2 mL) of the sugar over ½ cup (125 mL) very warm water in small bowl; stir until yeast is dissolved. Let stand until mixture is bubbly.

2. Place 1½ cups (375 mL) of the flour and ¼ teaspoon (1 mL) salt in medium bowl; stir in yeast mixture and 1 tablespoon (15 mL) of the oil, stirring until a smooth, soft dough forms. Knead on floured surface, using as much of the remaining flour as needed to form stiff elastic dough. Let dough rise covered in greased bowl in warm place until doubled in bulk, 30 to 45 minutes.

3. While dough is rising, make sauce. Finely chop undrained tomatoes in can with scissors or knife. Chop onion. Mince garlic. Heat remaining 1 tablespoon (15 mL) oil in medium saucepan over medium heat. Add onion; cook until soft, about 5 minutes. Add garlic; cook 30 seconds. Add tomatoes, tomato paste, oregano, basil, remaining ½ teaspoon (2 mL) sugar, remaining ½ teaspoon (2 mL) salt and the black pepper. Heat to boiling; reduce heat to medium-low. Simmer uncov-

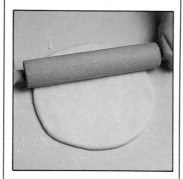

ered, stirring occasionally, until sauce is thick, 10 to 15 minutes. Transfer sauce to bowl; let cool.

4. Heat oven to 450°F (230°C). Punch dough down. Knead briefly on lightly floured surface to distribute air bubbles; let dough rest 5 minutes. Flatten dough into circle on lightly floured surface. Roll out dough, starting at center and rolling to edges, into 10-inch (25 cm) circle. Place circle in greased 12-inch (30 cm) pizza pan; pat dough out to edges of pan. Let stand covered 15 minutes.

5. Meanwhile, core and seed red and green peppers; cut into ¾-inch (2 cm) pieces. Cut olives in half. Trim mushrooms; wipe clean with damp kitchen towel. Cut mushrooms into thin slices. Drain anchovies. Mix mozzarella and Parmesan cheeses in small bowl. Spread sauce evenly over pizza dough. Sprinkle with two-thirds of the cheeses. Arrange peppers, olives, mushrooms, and anchovies on top of pizza.

6. Sprinkle remaining cheeses on top of pizza. Bake until crust is golden brown, about 20 minutes. Cut into wedges to serve.

Makes 4 to 6 servings.

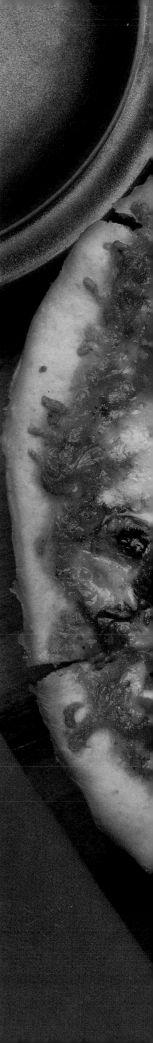

Fish & Shellfish

Fried Smelts

Herbed Butter
½ cup (125 mL) butter
1 tablespoon (15 mL) minced
  fresh parsley
1 green onion, minced
1 clove garlic, minced
Pinch each salt and pepper

Fried Smelts
3 to 4 dozen fresh smelts*
¾ cup (180 mL) all-purpose
  flour
1½ teaspoons (7 mL) salt
¼ teaspoon (1 mL) pepper
2 large eggs
¼ cup (60 mL) milk
2½ cups (625 mL) soft fresh
  breadcrumbs
¼ cup (60 mL) butter
¼ cup (60 mL) vegetable oil
Lemon wedges

Note: *In Italy, this preparation is commonly done with fresh sardines. Try this dish with scaled fresh sardines if they are available in your area.

1. For Herbed Butter: Beat butter in small bowl until smooth and creamy. Stir in parsley, green onion, garlic, salt and pepper. Let stand covered at room temperature 30 minutes to blend flavors.

2. For Fried Smelts: Cut off heads of smelts with knife; discard. Cut undersides of smelts open with scissors; clean insides of smelts.

3. Spread smelts open. Cut through backbones at tail end with scissors as shown. Starting at tail end, gently pull backbones out; discard. Rinse smelts under gently running cold water. Drain smelts; pat dry with paper towels.

4. Mix flour, salt and pepper in shallow dish or on waxed paper. Beat eggs and milk in second dish. Place breadcrumbs in third dish.

5. Dip smelts in flour mixture to coat both sides evenly. Dip smelts in egg mixture, then in bread crumbs to coat evenly; place in single layer on tray.

6. Heat ¼ cup (60 mL) butter and oil in large skillet over medium heat. Add as many smelts as will fit in single layer without crowding. Cook uncovered, turning once, until deep golden brown and cooked through, about 2 minutes per side. Repeat until all smelts are cooked. Serve with lemon wedges and Herbed Butter.

Makes 4 entree servings or 8 first course servings.

Fritto Misto

1 cup (250 mL) all-purpose
   flour
½ teaspoon (2 mL) salt
⅛ teaspoon (0.5 mL) white
   pepper
Large pinch cayenne pepper
1 cup (250 mL) warm water
1 tablespoon (15 mL) olive
   oil
1 pound (450 g) squid
1 pound (450 g) large
   shrimp, shelled and
   deveined
½ pound (225 g) fresh
   scallops cut into 1-inch
   (2.5 cm) pieces
½ pound (225 g) firm white
   fish fillets, such as
   haddock or flounder, cut
   into 2 × 1-inch (5 × 2.5 cm)
   pieces
Vegetable oil
2 large egg whites, at room
   temperature
Lemon wedges
Tartar Sauce (recipe below)

1. Combine flour, salt, white
pepper and cayenne pepper in
medium bowl; stir to mix well.
Combine 1 cup (250 mL) warm
water and the olive oil; stir into
flour mixture. Whisk until
smooth. Let batter stand
covered, at room temperature,
1 hour.

2. Meanwhile, clean and slice
squid following directions for
Marinated Calamari (see Index
for recipe). Pat squid and all
other seafood thoroughly dry
with paper towels.

3. Heat 1½ inches (4 cm)
vegetable oil in large saucepan
to 375°F (190°C). While oil is
heating, beat egg whites in
small mixer bowl until stiff but
not dry peaks form; fold into
batter until smooth. Heat oven
to 200°F (95°C).

4. Dip a few pieces of seafood
into batter to coat well; let
excess batter drip off. Fry in
oil, turning once or twice, until
golden, 1½ to 2 minutes. (*Caution:* Squid will pop and
spatter during frying; stand at
arm's length from pan.) Remove from oil with slotted
spoon. Drain on paper towel-
lined rack; keep warm in oven.
Repeat until all seafood has
been fried. Serve at once with
lemon wedges and Tartar
Sauce.

Makes 6 servings.

Tartar Sauce

2 large egg yolks, at room
   temperature*
1 tablespoon (15 mL) fresh
   lemon juice
1 teaspoon (5 mL) white
   wine vinegar
1 teaspoon (5 mL)
   Dijon-style mustard
½ teaspoon (2 mL) salt
Pinch white pepper
1 cup (250 mL) vegetable oil,
   at room temperature
1 green onion
1 tablespoon (15 mL) drained
   capers
1 small sweet gherkin
2 tablespoons (30 mL)
   chopped fresh parsley

Note: *Mayonnaise can be
made in blender or food processor, if desired. Substitute 1
whole egg for the egg yolks
and follow manufacturer's instructions for mixing mayonnaise.

1. To make mayonnaise, bowl
must be at room temperature;
if bowl is cold, fill with hot
water, then empty bowl and
dry thoroughly. Combine egg
yolks, lemon juice, vinegar,

mustard, salt and pepper in
medium bowl; whisk until
smooth. Add half the oil, drop
by drop, whisking continuously, to thoroughly incorpo-
rate oil. Whisking continuously, add remaining oil in
slow steady stream.

2. Trim and thinly slice green
onion. Mince capers and gherkin. Fold green onion, capers,
gherkin and parsley into
mayonnaise. Refrigerate covered until ready to serve. Serve
with Fritto Misto (recipe above),
Fried Calamari (see Index for
recipe) or other fried fish
dishes.

**Makes about 1⅓ cups
(330 mL).**

Fish with Zucchini

2 small zucchini
1 can (14½ ounces or 415 g) whole peeled tomatoes
1 pound (450 g) skinned red snapper, cod or striped bass fillets
¼ cup (60 mL) plus 1 tablespoon (15 mL) butter
2 tablespoons (30 mL) olive oil
1 tablespoon (15 mL) chopped fresh basil or ¾ teaspoon (4 mL) dried basil, crumbled
½ teaspoon (2 mL) salt
1 sprig fresh rosemary or ¼ teaspoon (1 mL) dried rosemary, crumbled
⅛ teaspoon (0.5 mL) pepper
2 tablespoons (30 mL) fine dry unseasoned breadcrumbs
2 teaspoons (10 mL) lemon juice

1. Heat oven to 400°F (200°C). Cut zucchini crosswise into ¼-inch- (0.5 cm) thick slices. Press tomatoes and their liquid through sieve into bowl; discard seeds. Pat fish dry.

2. Heat ¼ cup (60 mL) of the butter in 12-inch (30 cm) non-corrosive skillet over medium-high heat; when foam subsides, reduce heat to medium. Add fish fillets; cook, turning once, until fish is light brown, 1 to 2 minutes per side. Remove fish with slotted spatula to greased shallow baking dish.

3. Add oil to butter remaining in skillet; increase heat to medium-high. Add zucchini; cook and stir until light brown, about 3 minutes. Stir in half the basil, the salt, rosemary and pepper; cook 30 seconds. Stir in sieved tomatoes. Heat to boiling; reduce heat to medium. Cook uncovered, stirring frequently, until sauce is slightly thickened, about 5 minutes. (Remove and discard rosemary at this point if using fresh).

4. Spoon zucchini-tomato mixture over fish in baking dish. Sprinkle with breadcrumbs and remaining basil. Drizzle lemon juice over crumbs; dot with remaining 1 tablespoon (15 mL) butter. Bake uncovered just until fish is cooked through and topping is light brown, 10 to 15 minutes.

Makes 2 to 3 servings.

Fish Milanese

⅓ cup (80 mL) plus 2 tablespoons (30 mL) olive oil
2 tablespoons (30 mL) lemon juice
½ teaspoon (2 mL) salt
Pinch pepper
1 small onion, finely chopped
1 pound (450 g) flounder or haddock fillets (4 to 8 pieces)
2 large eggs
1 tablespoon (15 mL) milk
¾ cup (180 mL) fine dry unseasoned breadcrumbs
½ cup (125 mL) all-purpose flour
¼ cup (60 mL) plus 2 tablespoons (30 mL) butter
1 small clove garlic, minced
1 tablespoon (15 mL) chopped fresh parsley
Lemon wedges

1. Whisk ⅓ cup (80 mL) of the oil, the lemon juice, salt and pepper in small bowl; stir in onion. Transfer marinade to noncorrosive baking dish.

2. Rinse fish; pat dry with paper towels. Place fish in marinade in baking dish; spoon marinade over fish to coat thoroughly. Refrigerate covered, turning fish over occasionally, 1 hour.

3. Whisk eggs and milk in shallow bowl. Spread breadcrumbs on plate. Spread flour on waxed paper or on plate. Remove fish from marinade; pat dry with paper towels. Discard marinade.

4. Dip fish to coat both sides evenly, first in flour, then in eggs, then in breadcrumbs. Press crumb coating firmly onto fish. Place on waxed paper; refrigerate 15 minutes.

5. Heat 2 tablespoons (30 mL) of the butter and remaining 2 tablespoons (30 mL) oil in large skillet over medium heat. When foam subsides, add fish. Cook, turning once, until fish is golden brown and cooked through, 2 to 3 minutes per side. Remove to plate.

6. Melt remaining ¼ cup (60 mL) butter in medium skillet over medium heat. Add garlic. Cook until butter turns light brown, 1 to 2 minutes; stir in parsley. Pour browned butter over fish. Serve at once with lemon wedges.

Makes 3 to 4 servings.

Marinated Calamari

1 pound (450 g) fresh or
  thawed frozen squid
⅓ cup (80 mL) olive oil
¼ cup (60 mL) fresh lemon
  juice
1 small clove garlic, minced
1 tablespoon (15 mL)
  chopped fresh parsley
1 tablespoon (15 mL)
  chopped fresh basil or ½
  teaspoon (2 mL) dried
  basil, crumbled
¼ teaspoon (0.5 mL) salt
Pinch white pepper

1. To clean squid, work in sink. Hold body of squid firmly in one hand; grasp head firmly with other hand; pull head, twisting gently from side to side. Head and contents of body should come away in one piece. Cut tentacles off head; reserve. Discard head and contents of body.

Grasp tip of pointed, thin, clear cartilage protruding from body; pull out and discard.

2. Rinse squid under cold running water. Peel off and discard spotted outer membrane. Pull off side fins; reserve. Rinse inside of squid bodies thoroughly under running water to remove any grit or extraneous matter. Cut squid

bodies crosswise into ¼-inch (0.5 cm) rings. Cut reserved fins into thin slices. Body rings, fins and reserved tentacles are all edible parts.

3. Drop squid pieces into large saucepan of boiling water; reduce heat to medium. Cook uncovered until squid is tender, about 15 minutes.

4. Meanwhile, mix oil and lemon juice in medium bowl. Remove squid from water with skimmer or slotted spoon, draining well. Add to oil mixture; stir to coat. Refrigerate covered, stirring occasionally, 12 to 24 hours.

5. Stir remaining ingredients into squid mixture. Refrigerate covered 2 to 4 hours. Serve in the marinade.

Makes 2 to 3 servings.

Fried Calamari

1 pound (450 g) fresh or
  thawed frozen squid
1 large egg
1 tablespoon (15 mL) milk
¾ cup (180 mL) fine dry
  unseasoned breadcrumbs
Vegetable oil
Tartar Sauce, if desired (see
  Index for recipe)
Lemon wedges

1. Clean and slice squid following directions for Marinated Calamari (see above). Pat squid pieces thoroughly dry with paper towels.

2. Beat egg with milk in small bowl. Add squid pieces; stir to

coat well. Remove a few squid pieces from egg mixture and place in single layer on breadcrumbs. Turn pieces over to coat evenly with crumbs. Place coated squid in shallow bowl or on plate. Repeat process to coat all squid. Let stand 10 to 15 minutes before frying.

3. To deep-fry squid, heat 1½ inches (4 cm) oil in large saucepan to 350°F (180°C). (**Caution:** Squid will pop and spatter during frying; stand at arm's length from pan.) Fry 8 to 10 pieces of squid at a time in hot oil until light brown, 45 to 60 seconds. Remove with slotted spoon to paper towel-lined rack.

4. Squid can be shallow-fried, if desired; this method uses less oil but requires slightly more hand-work. Heat about 3/16 inch (0.5 cm) oil in large skillet over medium-high heat

until hot; reduce heat to medium. (**Caution:** Squid will pop and spatter during frying; stand at arm's length from pan.) Add as many pieces of squid as will fit in single layer without crowding. Cook, turning once with 2 forks, until light brown on both sides, 1 to 1½ minutes. Remove with slotted spoon to paper towel-lined rack. Repeat until all squid have been fried.

5. Serve hot with Tartar Sauce and lemon wedges.

Makes 2 to 3 servings.

Osso Buco

8 pieces veal shank, cut 2 to 2½ inches (5 to 6.5 cm) thick (about 6½ pounds or 2925 g)
5 tablespoons (75 mL) butter
2 medium carrots, pared and diced
2 stalks celery, chopped
2 medium onions, chopped
1 medium clove garlic, minced
¾ cup (180 mL) all-purpose flour
2 tablespoons (30 mL) olive oil
1 cup (250 mL) dry white wine
1 can (14½ ounces or 415 g) whole peeled tomatoes
1½ cups (375 mL) beef broth
1 teaspoon (5 mL) dried basil, crumbled
½ teaspoon (2 mL) dried rosemary, crumbled
¼ teaspoon (1 mL) dried thyme, crumbled
1 bay leaf
¼ teaspoon (1 mL) salt
⅛ teaspoon (0.5 mL) pepper
1 medium clove garlic, minced
3 tablespoons (45 mL) minced fresh parsley
1 teaspoon (5 mL) grated lemon peel

1. Tie any loose veal shanks around circumference with kitchen twine.

2. Heat 3 tablespoons (45 mL) of the butter in large skillet over medium heat. When foam subsides, add carrots, celery and onions; sauté just until onions begin to color, 7 to 8 minutes. Add 1 clove garlic; cook 30 seconds. Transfer mix-

ture to wide shallow non-corrosive Dutch oven.

3. Roll veal shanks in flour to coat lightly. Heat oil and remaining 2 tablespoons (30 mL) butter in large skillet over medium heat; add shanks. Cook, turning occasionally, until shanks are brown on all sides; remove shanks to paper towel-lined tray.

4. Add wine to skillet. Cook over medium heat, scraping up brown bits that cling to bottom and sides of pan, 1 minute. Remove from heat. Press tomatoes and their liquid through sieve into skillet. Stir in broth, basil, rosemary,

thyme, bay leaf, salt and pepper.

5. Arrange veal shanks upright on top of vegetables in Dutch oven. Pour in tomato-wine mixture. Heat to boiling on high heat; reduce heat to very low. Simmer covered, basting shanks with cooking liquid occasionally, until veal is very tender, 1½ to 2 hours. Remove shanks from Dutch oven to deep serving dish. Cook and stir sauce over high heat, until slightly thickened; pour over shanks. Mix 1 clove garlic, parsley, and lemon peel. Sprinkle over shanks.

Makes 8 servings.

Veal Florentine

6 ounces (170 g) fresh spinach
Warm salted water
6 tablespoons (90 mL) butter
1 can (14½ ounces or 415 g) whole peeled tomatoes
2 cloves garlic, minced
¼ cup (60 mL) dry white wine
¼ cup (60 mL) water
1 tablespoon (15 mL) tomato paste
½ teaspoon (2 mL) sugar
¾ teaspoon (4 mL) salt
¼ teaspoon (1 mL) pepper
¼ cup (60 mL) all-purpose flour
4 veal cutlets, cut ⅜-inch (1 cm) thick, about 4 ounces (115 g) each
1 tablespoon (15 mL) olive oil
4 slices mozzarella cheese (1 ounce or 30 g each)

1. Rinse spinach in large basin of warm salted water to remove sand; drain. Trim stems. Stack leaves; cut crosswise into coarse shreds. Place spinach with water that clings to leaves in medium saucepan over medium heat. Steam covered, stirring occasionally, until tender, about 4 minutes. Add 2 tablespoons (30 mL) of the butter; cook and stir uncovered until butter is absorbed. Remove spinach from pan. Reserve.

2. Press tomatoes and their liquid through sieve into bowl; discard seeds. Heat 2 tablespoons (30 mL) of the remaining butter in medium saucepan over medium heat. Add garlic; sauté 30 seconds. Add sieved tomatoes, the wine, ¼ cup (60 mL) water, the tomato paste, sugar, ½ teaspoon (2 mL) of the salt and ⅛ teaspoon (0.5 mL) of the pepper to pan. Heat to boiling; reduce heat to low. Simmer uncovered, stirring occasionally, 10 minutes. Remove from heat.

3. Mix flour and remaining ¼ teaspoon (1 mL) salt and ⅛ teaspoon (0.5 mL) pepper in small bag. Pound veal cutlets until

¼-inch (0.5 cm) or less thick. Pat dry with paper toweling. Shake one piece of veal at a time in seasoned flour in bag to coat evenly. Heat oil and remaining 2 tablespoons (30 mL) butter in large noncorrosive skillet over medium heat. Add veal to skillet; cook, turning once, until light brown, 2 to 3 minutes per side. Remove from heat. Spoon off excess fat. Top veal with reserved spinach, dividing evenly; top each with 1 slice of cheese.

4. Pour tomato sauce into skillet around veal; do not let sauce cover cheese. Lift edges of veal to let sauce flow under. Cook uncovered over medium heat until sauce is bubbly; reduce heat to very low. Barely simmer covered 8 minutes. Serve at once.

Makes 4 servings.

Chicken Marsala

2 tablespoons (30 mL) unsalted butter
1 tablespoon (15 mL) vegetable oil
4 skinned boned chicken breast halves (about 1¼ pounds or 565 g)
4 slices mozzarella cheese (1 ounce or 30 g each)
12 capers, drained
4 flat anchovy fillets, drained
1 tablespoon (15 mL) chopped fresh parsley
1 clove garlic, minced
3 tablespoons (45 mL) marsala
⅔ cup (160 mL) whipping cream
Pinch salt
Pinch pepper

1. Heat butter and oil in 10-inch (25 cm) skillet over medium-high heat. When foam subsides, add chicken; reduce heat to medium. Cook uncovered, turning once, until chicken is deep golden brown on both sides and cooked through, 5 to 6 minutes per side. Remove chicken from skillet to board. Top each chicken piece with one cheese slice, 3 capers and 1 anchovy fillet.

2. Return chicken to skillet. Sprinkle with parsley. Cook covered over low heat just until cheese is semi-melted, about 3 minutes. Remove chicken from pan to heated serving platter. Keep warm.

3. Add garlic to drippings in skillet; sauté over medium heat 30 seconds. Stir in marsala; cook, stirring and scraping up brown bits which cling to bottom and sides of skillet, 45 seconds. Stir in cream. Cook uncovered, stirring constantly, until sauce is slightly thickened, about 3 minutes. Stir in salt and pepper. Spoon sauce over chicken. (Serve with buttered new potatoes and green vegetable, if desired.)

Makes 4 servings.

Veal Scallopine

4 veal cutlets, cut ⅜-inch (1 cm) thick, about 4 ounces (115 g) each
½ pound (225 g) fresh mushrooms, thinly sliced
¼ cup (60 mL) butter
2 tablespoons (30 mL) olive oil
1 small onion, finely chopped
¼ cup (60 mL) dry sherry
2 teaspoons (10 mL) all-purpose flour
½ cup (125 mL) beef broth
¼ teaspoon (1 mL) salt
⅛ teaspoon (0.5 mL) pepper
2 tablespoons (30 mL) whipping cream

1. Pound veal cutlets until ¼-inch (0.5 cm) or less thick. Pat dry with paper toweling.

2. Sauté mushrooms in butter in 12-inch (30 cm) skillet over medium heat until light brown, 3 to 4 minutes. Remove mushrooms with slotted spoon to bowl; reserve.

3. Add oil to butter remaining in skillet; heat over medium heat. Add veal; cook, turning once, until light brown, 2 to 3 minutes per side. Remove veal to plate; reserve. Add onion to skillet; sauté until tender, 2 to 3 minutes.

4. Stir sherry into onion in skillet. Heat over medium-high heat to boiling; boil 15 seconds. Stir in flour; cook, stirring constantly, 30 seconds. Remove from heat; stir in broth. Cook uncovered over medium heat, stirring constantly, to boiling. Stir reserved mushrooms, the salt and pepper into sauce. Add reserved veal to sauce; reduce heat to low. Simmer covered until veal is tender, about 8 minutes. Remove from heat.

5. Push veal to one side of skillet. Stir cream into sauce, mixing well. Heat over low heat just until heated through. Serve immediately—with Pasta with Oil & Garlic (see Index for recipe), if desired.

Makes 4 servings.

Venetian Liver with Onions

3 large onions
2 tablespoons (30 mL) butter
3 tablespoons (45 mL) olive oil
1½ pounds (675 g) calf's liver, cut into ½-inch- (1.5 cm) thick pieces
⅓ cup (80 mL) all-purpose flour
2 tablespoons (30 mL) chopped fresh parsley
½ teaspoon (2 mL) salt
Pinch pepper

1. Cut onions crosswise into ⅛-inch- (0.5 cm) thick slices. Heat butter and 2 tablespoons (30 mL) of the oil in 12-inch (30 cm) heavy skillet over medium heat; when foam subsides, reduce heat to medium-low. Add onions; cook uncovered, stirring frequently, until onions are limp and golden, 15 to 20 minutes. (Onions can be cooked to light brown, if desired, a few minutes longer.) Remove from heat.

2. While onions are cooking, rinse liver under cold running water; drain and pat dry with paper toweling. Cut off and discard thin skin around edge of pieces; cut out and discard any large veins. Cut liver pieces into thin strips, approximately 3 × ½ × ¼ inches (8 × 1.5 × 0.5 cm).

3. Place liver in sieve or colander; add flour. Toss liver very gently with 2 spoons to coat evenly with flour. Shake sieve to remove excess flour.

4. Remove onions from skillet to bowl with slotted spoon, draining well. Add remaining 1 tablespoon (15 mL) oil to oil and butter remaining in skillet; heat over high heat until very hot.

5. Add liver to skillet; cook uncovered over high heat just until liver is light brown on bottom, about 1 minute. Turn liver over; cook second side 1 minute. Stir in onions; cook just until liver has lost its red color inside and is firm but not tough, 1 to 2 minutes longer. Do not overcook. Immediately remove from heat; stir in parsley, salt and pepper. Serve at once.

Makes 4 servings.

Vitello Tonnato

1 can (2 ounces or 60 g) flat anchovy fillets
1 medium clove garlic
1 lean boneless veal roast, such as leg of veal or top round (2½ to 3 pounds or 1125 to 1350 g), rolled and tied
1 large carrot, pared
1 large stalk celery
1 large onion
4 cups (1 L) water
1½ cups (375 mL) dry white wine
1 large egg
4½ tablespoons (67 mL) fresh lemon juice
½ teaspoon (2 mL) salt
1 cup (250 mL) vegetable oil
1½ tablespoons (22 mL) drained capers
1 can (7 ounces or 200 g) tuna in olive oil
⅔ cup (160 mL) olive oil
1 large egg yolk
Large pinch white pepper
1 tablespoon (15 mL) chopped fresh parsley
Curly endive, ripe olives and sieved hard-cooked egg yolks, if desired

1. Drain 3 anchovies; cut into ½-inch (1.5 cm) pieces. Cut garlic into thin slivers. With paring knife, cut 1-inch- (2.5 cm) deep slits in top of veal at 1-inch (2.5 cm) intervals. Push a piece of anchovy and garlic into each slit with finger.

2. Cut carrot, celery and onion into quarters; place in large Dutch oven. Add 4 cups (1 L) water and the wine. Heat covered to boiling. Add veal; reduce heat to very low. Simmer veal covered until tender, 1½ to 2 hours. Let veal cool in broth; then refrigerate in broth, covered, overnight.

3. About 4 hours before serving, combine whole egg, 1½ tablespoons (22 mL) of the lemon juice, the salt and ¼ cup (60 mL) of the vegetable oil in blender container; process on medium speed until blended. With motor running, add remaining vegetable oil in thin steady stream. Transfer mayonnaise to large bowl. (To

make mayonnaise in food processor, follow manufacturer's directions.) Drain remaining anchovies. Chop capers. Combine anchovies, undrained tuna, the olive oil, egg yolk, pepper and remaining lemon juice in blender (or food processor); process on medium speed until smooth. Stir tuna mixture into mayonnaise. Stir in capers and parsley.

4. Remove veal from broth; discard broth. Cut veal crosswise into ³⁄₁₆-inch- (0.5 cm) thick slices. Spread a generous layer of tuna sauce in bottom of large platter; top with a flat layer of veal slices. Coat veal with generous layer of tuna sauce. Arrange remaining veal slices overlapping each other on top of first layer of veal; spread with generous amount of tuna sauce to cover veal completely. Refrigerate at least 3 hours before serving. Refrigerate any remaining sauce separately. Garnish platter with endive, olives and sieved egg yolk. Serve with remaining sauce.

Makes 8 to 10 servings.

Veal Parmesan

1 small red bell pepper, finely chopped
1 medium onion, finely chopped
1 stalk celery, finely chopped
1 clove garlic, minced
4 tablespoons (60 mL) olive oil
1 can (14½ ounces or 415 g) whole peeled tomatoes, undrained, finely chopped
1 cup (250 mL) chicken broth
1 tablespoon (15 mL) tomato paste
1 tablespoon (15 mL) chopped fresh parsley
1 teaspoon (5 mL) sugar
¾ teaspoon (4 mL) dried basil, crumbled
½ teaspoon (2 mL) salt
⅛ teaspoon (0.5 mL) pepper
4 veal cutlets, cut ⅜-inch (1 cm) thick, about 4 ounces (115 g) each
1 large egg
¼ cup (60 mL) all-purpose flour
⅔ cup (160 mL) fine dry unseasoned breadcrumbs

2 tablespoons (30 mL) butter
1½ cups (375 mL) shredded mozarella cheese
⅔ cup (160 mL) freshly grated Parmesan cheese

1. Sauté bell pepper, onion, celery and garlic in 1 tablespoon (15 mL) of the oil in medium noncorrosive saucepan over medium heat 5 minutes. Stir in tomatoes, broth, tomato paste, parsley, sugar, basil, salt and pepper. Simmer covered over low heat 20 minutes. Uncover pan; cook over medium heat, stirring frequently, until sauce is very thick, about 20 minutes longer.

2. Pound veal until ¼-inch (0.5 cm) thick. Pat dry with paper toweling. Beat egg in shallow bowl; spread flour and breadcrumbs on separate plates. Dip veal to coat both sides evenly, first in flour, then in egg, then in breadcrumbs. Heat butter and 2 tablespoons (30 mL) of the remaining oil in

12-inch (30 cm) skillet over medium-high heat. Add veal. Cook, turning once, until light brown, 2 to 3 minutes per side.

3. Heat oven to 350°F (180°C). Remove veal from skillet with slotted spatula to shallow baking dish. Sprinkle mozzarella cheese evenly over veal. Spoon tomato sauce evenly over cheese. Sprinkle Parmesan cheese evenly over tomato sauce.

4. Drizzle remaining 1 tablespoon (15 mL) oil over Parmesan cheese. Bake uncovered until veal is tender and cheese topping is golden brown, about 25 minutes.

Makes 4 servings.

Chicken Cacciatore

1 broiler-fryer chicken, 3 to
   3½ pounds (1350 to
   1600 g), cut up into
   8 pieces
1 tablespoon (15 mL) olive
   oil
4 ounces (115 g) fresh
   mushrooms, finely
   chopped
1 medium onion, chopped
1 medium clove garlic,
   minced
½ cup (125 mL) dry white
   wine
1½ tablespoons (22 mL)
   white wine vinegar
½ cup (125 mL) chicken
   broth
1 teaspoon (5 mL) dried
   basil, crumbled
½ teaspoon (2 mL) dried
   marjoram, crumbled
½ teaspoon (2 mL) salt
⅛ teaspoon (0.5 mL) pepper
1 can (14½ ounces or 415 g)
   whole peeled tomatoes
8 Italian- or Greek-style
   black olives
1 tablespoon (15 mL)
   chopped fresh parsley

1. Rinse chicken; drain and pat dry. Heat oil in large non-corrosive skillet over medium heat. Add as many chicken pieces as will fit in single layer without crowding. Cook, turning once, until chicken is brown, about 8 minutes per side; remove chicken to flameproof casserole or Dutch oven. Repeat until all chicken has been browned.

2. Add mushrooms and onion to drippings remaining in skillet. Sauté over medium heat until onion is soft, about 5 mintues. Add garlic; sauté 30 seconds. Add wine and vinegar to skillet; cook over medium-high heat until liquid is almost completely evaporated, about 5 minutes. Stir in chicken broth, basil, marjoram, salt and pepper. Remove from heat.

3. Press tomatoes and their liquid through sieve into bowl; discard seeds. Stir sieved tomatoes into onion mixture in skillet. Heat to boiling; boil uncovered 2 minutes.

4. Pour tomato-onion mixture over chicken. Heat to boiling, reduce heat to low. Simmer covered until chicken is tender, about 25 minutes. Remove chicken pieces to serving dish, keep warm.

5. Heat tomato-onion mixture to boiling; boil uncovered over medium-high heat 5 minutes. Cut olives in half, remove and discard pits. Add olives and parsley to sauce; cook 1 minute longer. Pour sauce over chicken and serve.

Makes 4 servings.

Veal Casserole

¼ pound (115 g) sliced
   pancetta*
1 fennel bulb
½ pound (225 g) fresh
   medium mushrooms
3 small onions
6 veal loin chops, ¾-inch
   (2 cm) thick, or 2½
   pounds (1125 g) veal
   shoulder steaks, ¾-inch
   (2 cm) thick
3 medium cloves garlic
3 tablespoons (45 mL) butter
1 tablespoon (15 mL) olive
   oil
1 cup (250 mL) chicken broth
¾ cup (180 mL) dry white
   wine
1 tablespoon (15 mL) tomato
   paste
1 teaspoon (5 mL) salt
⅛ teaspoon (0.5 mL) pepper
1½ tablespoons (22 mL)
   all-purpose flour
1½ tablespoons (22 mL) cold
   water

*Note: *Pancetta, an unsmoked, cured bacon, is available in Italian delicatessens. If necessary, use American bacon.*

1. Cut pancetta into 1-inch (2.5 cm) pieces. Trim bottom end of fennel bulb and cut off stalks; discard. Cut fennel bulb lengthwise in half, then slice crosswise. Clean and trim mushrooms; cut into quarters. Quarter onions. Trim any fat or gristle from veal. Mince garlic.

2. Heat oven to 325°F (160°C). Heat butter and oil in large skillet over medium heat. Add veal in single layer; cook until deep brown, about 4 minutes per side. Remove veal to large shallow casserole.

3. Add pancetta to drippings in skillet. Sauté over medium heat 3 minutes. Add onions, fennel, mushrooms and garlic; sauté until onions are light brown, about 5 minutes. Add broth, wine, tomato paste, salt and pepper. Heat to boiling, stirring and scraping up brown bits which cling to bottom and sides of skillet.

4. Pour vegetable-broth mixture over veal in casserole. Bake covered until veal is tender, 30 to 45 minutes. Remove veal from casserole to deep, heatproof serving dish; keep warm. Transfer vegetable-broth mixture back to skillet. Mix flour and water in cup until smooth. Stir into vegetable mixture; cook, stirring constantly, over medium heat until sauce thickens and bubbles for 1 mintue. Pour vegetable sauce over veal. Serve at once.

Makes 4 to 6 servings.

Salads & Vegetables

Calamari & Vegetable Salad

1 can (2 ounces or 60 g) flat anchovy fillets
1 tablespoon (15 mL) chopped fresh parsley
3 tablespoons (45 mL) olive oil
2 small cloves garlic
1 large ripe avocado
1 tablespoon (15 mL) white wine vinegar
1 large green bell pepper
2 large ripe tomatoes
8 Italian- or Greek-style black olives
2 teaspoons (10 mL) chopped fresh basil or ¾ teaspoon (4 mL) dried basil, crumbled
1 teaspoon (5 mL) dried oregano, crumbled
¼ teaspoon (1 mL) salt
⅛ teaspoon (0.5 mL) pepper
1 small cucumber
½ small head iceberg lettuce
Fried Calamari (see Index for recipe)

1. Drain anchovies and discard liquid. Combine anchovies, parsley and 1 tablespoon (15 mL) of the olive oil in small bowl. Crush 1 of the garlic cloves through a press into bowl; stir to mix. Reserve mixture at room temperature until you assemble salad.

2. Pare and pit avocado. Cut lengthwise into ½-inch- (1.5 cm) wide slices; cut slices crosswise in thirds. Toss avocado with vinegar in large bowl.

3. Core and seed bell pepper; cut into thin slices and add to avocado in bowl. Cut each tomato into 6 wedges; add to bowl. Add olives, basil, oregano, salt and pepper to bowl. Crush remaining garlic clove; add to bowl.

4. Cut cucumber crosswise into thin slices. Add to avocado mixture in bowl. Drizzle remaining 2 tablespoons (30 mL) oil over mixture; toss gently to mix.

5. Break lettuce into small pieces; place in bottom of salad bowl. Spoon avocado mixture in even layer over lettuce. Refrigerate covered until serving time.

6. Prepare Fried Calamari.

7. Just before serving, arrange Fried Calamari in a border on top of salad. Arrange reserved anchovies in center of salad; drizzle anchovy marinade over salad.

Makes 4 to 6 servings.

Radicchio & Fennel Salad

11 Italian- or Greek-style
  black olives
¼ cup (60 mL) olive oil
1 tablespoon (15 mL) fresh
  lemon juice
1 flat anchovy fillet or ½
  teaspoon (2 mL) anchovy
  paste
¼ teaspoon (1 mL) salt
Large pinch pepper
Large pinch sugar
1 fresh fennel bulb
1 head radicchio*

Note: *Radicchio, a tart red chicory, is available in some Italian and specialty food shops. If not available, 2 heads of Belgian endive can be used; although it does not provide the dramatic red color, it will give a similar texture and its slightly bitter flavor will interplay well with the robust dressing and the sweet anise-bite of the fennel.

1. For dressing: Pit 3 of the olives; discard pits. Place pitted olives, the oil, lemon juice and anchovy in blender or food processor; process 5 seconds. Add salt, pepper and sugar; process until olives are finely chopped, about 5 seconds longer. Reserve.

2. Cut off and discard fennel stalks. Cut off and discard root end at base of fennel bulb and any discolored parts of bulb. Cut fennel bulb lengthwise into 8 wedges; separate segments of each wedge.

3. Separate radicchio leave rinse thoroughly in large bas of water. Drain well.

4. Arrange radicchio leave fennel and remaining olives o serving plate. Spoon dressin over salad. Serve immediatel

Makes 3 to 4 servings.

Vegetable Salad

3½ tablespoons (52 mL)
  white wine vinegar
1½ teaspoons (7 mL) minced
  fresh basil or ½ teaspoon
  (2 mL) dried basil,
  crumbled
½ teaspoon (2 mL) salt
⅛ teaspoon (0.5 mL) pepper
Pinch sugar
6 tablespoons (90 mL) olive
  oil
2 medium ripe tomatoes
⅓ cup (80 mL) green olives
⅓ cup (80 mL) Italian- or
  Greek-style black olives
1 head leaf or red leaf lettuce
1 small head curly endive
2 heads Belgian endive

1. For dressing: Whisk vinegar, basil, salt, pepper and sugar in small bowl. Whisking continuously, add oil in slow steady stream; whisk until oil is thoroughly blended. Cut tomatoes into quarters.

2. Combine tomatoes and green and black olives in medium bowl. Add dressing; mix lightly. Let stand uncovered at room temperature, stirring occasionally, 30 minutes.

3. Meanwhile, rinse leaf lettuce and curly endive; drain well. Core Belgian endive and separate into leaves; rinse and drain well. Refrigerate greens until ready to assemble salad.

4. Arrange greens, petal-fashion, in large shallow serving bowl. Transfer tomatoes and olives with slotted spoon to center of greens. Spoon remaining dressing over greens. Serve at once or refrigerate covered up to 30 minutes.

Makes 6 servings.

Cauliflower Neapolitan

6 pitted or stuffed green
   olives
½ small onion
1 stalk celery
½ head cauliflower (about ¾
   pound or 340 g)
2 tablespoons (30 mL) fresh
   lemon juice
¼ teaspoon (1 mL) salt
Pinch pepper
⅓ cup (80 mL) olive oil
2 tablespoons (30 mL)
   chopped fresh parsley
½ teaspoon (2 mL) drained
   capers

1. Slice olives. Thinly slice onion. Chop celery. Reserve.

2. Rinse, core and cut cauliflower into 1-inch (2.5 cm) flowerets; place in large saucepan of boiling water. Cook uncovered for 5 minutes after water returns to boiling. Drain cauliflower; rinse under cold running water until cauliflower is completely cooled. Drain well; pat dry.

3. Whisk lemon juice, salt and pepper in medium bowl. Whisking continuously, add oil in slow steady stream; whisk until oil is thoroughly blended. Add reserved olives, onion and celery, the parsley and capers; stir to mix well. Stir in cauliflower. Serve at once or refrigerate covered up to 3 hours.

Makes about 2½ cups (625 mL); about 4 servings.

Tomato & Salami Salad

1 tablespoon (15 mL) fresh
   lemon juice
1 tablespoon (15 mL)
   chopped fresh parsley
1 tablespoon (15 mL)
   chopped fresh basil or 1
   teaspoon (5 mL) dried
   basil, crumbled
1 medium clove garlic,
   minced
½ teaspoon (2 mL) grated
   lemon peel
¼ teaspoon (1 mL) salt
⅛ teaspoon (0.5 mL) pepper
⅓ cup (80 mL) olive oil
4 ounces (115 g) hard salami,
   thinly sliced
3 large ripe tomatoes

1. For dressing: Whisk lemon juice, parsley, basil, garlic, lemon peel, salt and pepper in small bowl. Whisking continuously, add oil in slow steady stream; whisk until oil is thoroughly blended.

2. Spread salami slices out in large shallow bowl or casserole. Pour dressing over slices. Lift slices with fork to allow dressing to flow underneath. Let stand covered at room temperature, turning slices over once, 1 hour.

3. Cut tomatoes into ¼-inch- (0.5 cm) thick slices. Top each tomato slice with a salami slice and arrange overlapping on large platter. Drizzle any dressing remaining in bowl over slices.

Makes 6 to 8 servings.

Stuffed Tomatoes

4 large or 5 medium firm, ripe tomatoes
Salt
5 ounces (140 g) fresh spinach
⅓ cup (80 mL) uncooked long-grain rice
1 tablespoon (15 mL) plus 2 teaspoons (10 mL) olive oil
1 tablespoon (15 mL) pine nuts (pignolias)
1 small clove garlic
¼ teaspoon (1 mL) dried basil, crumbled
¼ teaspoon (1 mL) salt
Pinch pepper
⅓ cup (80 mL) grated Parmesan cheese
2 teaspoons (10 mL) butter

1. Cut ½-inch (1.5 cm) slice off top of each tomato and discard. Cut out core of each tomato; scoop out and discard seeds and liquid. Sprinkle insides of tomatoes lightly with salt. Let tomatoes drain, inverted, on paper towel-lined wire rack, while proceeding with recipe.

2. Rinse spinach thoroughly in large basin of lukewarm water; drain. Pinch off and discard stems. Place spinach with water that clings to leaves in

large saucepan over medium heat. Steam covered until spinach is tender, about 5 minutes; drain. Reserve.

3. Cook rice according to package directions until tender. Transfer to medium bowl. Reserve.

4. Heat 2 teaspoons (10 mL) of the oil in small skillet over medium-low heat; add pine nuts. Sauté until nuts are light brown, 30 to 45 seconds. Transfer nuts immediately to paper towel-lined plate to drain.

5. Heat oven to 350°F (180°C). Squeeze reserved spinach gently to remove excess moisture but do not squeeze very dry. Process spinach in blender or food processor until coarsely chopped. Add pine nuts; process 5 seconds.

6. Mince garlic; add to reserved rice. Add spinach mixture, basil, ¼ teaspoon (1 mL) salt, the pepper and remaining 1 tablespoon (15 mL) oil; stir to mix. Stir in cheese.

7. Spoon rice mixture into tomatoes, mounding slightly. Dot tops of rice filling with butter. Place tomatoes in greased shallow casserole. Bake just until tomatoes are tender but not soft, 15 to 20 minutes.

Makes 4 to 5 servings.

Fried Eggplant & Mozzarella

1 medium eggplant (about 1 pound or 450 g)
2 teaspoons (10 mL) salt
6 ounces (170 g) mozzarella cheese, in one piece
½ teaspoon (2 mL) active dry yeast
1½ cups (375 mL) very warm water (105°F to 115°F or 40°C to 46°C)
2 cups (500 mL) all-purpose flour
⅛ teaspoon (0.5 mL) pepper
4½ tablespoons (67 mL) olive oil
1½ teaspoons (7 mL) minced fresh basil or ½ teaspoon (2 mL) dried basil, crumbled
Vegetable oil
1 large egg white
Lemon wedges

1. Rinse eggplant; cut crosswise into ¼-inch- (0.5 cm) thick slices. Sprinkle slices with salt; stand slices on edge in colander. Let stand and drain in sink or over bowl 1 hour. Cut

cheese into ⅛-inch- (0.5 cm) thick slices; trim roughly to

diameter of eggplant slices. Reserve, wrapped in plastic.

2. Sprinkle yeast over the very warm water in medium bowl; stir until dissolved. Whisk in 1½ cups (375 mL) of the flour and the pepper until smooth. Reserve batter at room temperature 30 minutes.

3. Meanwhile, rinse eggplant and drain well; press slices between paper towels to extract moisture. Heat 1½ table-

spoons (22 mL) of the olive oil in 12-inch (30 cm) skillet over

medium-high heat; add as many eggplant slices as will fit in single layer. Cook, turning once, until slices are light brown, about 2 minutes per side; remove to paper towel-lined wire rack. Repeat, using remaining olive oil, until all eggplant slices are browned. Sprinkle cheese slices with basil. Place each cheese slice between 2 eggplant slices; press firmly together and dip in remaining flour to coat lightly.

4. Heat 1½ inches (4 cm) vegetable oil in large saucepan to

350°F (180°C). Beat egg white in small mixer bowl until stiff but not dry peaks form; fold into yeast batter. Dip one eggplant sandwich at a time into batter and gently shake off excess; place in hot oil. Fry 3 to 4 sandwiches at a time, turning once, until light brown, 1 to 2 minutes per side. Transfer to paper towel-lined rack to drain. Serve hot with lemon wedges.

Makes 4 to 6 servings.

Desserts

Ricotta Cake

**1 chocolate or devil's food
  2-layer cake mix**
**⅔ cup (160 mL) sliced
  blanched almonds (about
  2 ounces or 60 g)**
1 cup (250 mL) ricotta cheese
**½ cup (125 mL) plus 2
  tablespoons (30 mL) sugar**
**4 tablespoons (60 mL)
  orange-flavored liqueur**
**4 ounces (115 g) semisweet
  chocolate**
**1 ounce (30 g) preserved
  ginger or 2 tablespoons
  (30 mL) crystallized
  ginger**
6 red candied cherries
⅔ cup (160 mL) water
**½ cup (125 mL) unsalted
  butter, at room
  temperature**

1. Prepare cake mix according to package directions. Spoon batter into greased and floured 8-inch (20 cm) round cake pans. Bake according to pack-

age directions. Remove cake from pans; cool completely on wire racks. Only one cake layer is used in this dessert; freeze second layer for another use.

2. Heat oven to 350°F (180°C). Place almonds in small baking pan. Bake until light brown, 6 to 8 minutes; let cool. Reserve for garnish.

3. For filling: Press ricotta cheese through sieve into

medium mixer bowl. Beat in ¼ cup (60 mL) of the sugar and 2 tablespoons (30 mL) of the liqueur. Finely chop 1 ounce (30 g) of the chocolate, the ginger and cherries; stir into cheese mixture.

4. Combine ⅓ cup (80 mL) of the water, 2 tablespoons (30 mL) of the sugar and the remaining 2 tablespoons (30 mL) liqueur in small saucepan. Cook and stir over medium-high heat until sugar dissolves and syrup boils; reduce heat to low. Simmer uncovered 1 minute. Remove from heat; cool syrup to room temperature.

5. Cut cake horizontally with thin serrated knife into 3 even

layers. Brush top of each layer with a third of the cooled syrup. Place bottom layer on serving plate. Spread half the cheese filling evenly over bottom layer. Top with middle cake layer; spread with remaining filling. Top with remaining cake layer.

6. For icing: Melt remaining 3 ounces (85 g) chocolate in top of double boiler, stirring constantly, over simmering water.

Remove from simmering water; cool chocolate to room temperature. Meanwhile, heat remaining ⅓ cup (80 mL) water and remaining ¼ cup (60 mL) sugar in small saucepan over medium-high heat until sugar dissolves and syrup boils. Remove from heat; cool syrup to room temperature. Beat butter in medium mixer bowl until light and creamy. Beat in cooled syrup, 1 teaspoon (5 mL) at a time. Gradually beat in cooled chocolate; beat until smooth. Spread frosting on top and sides of cake. Press reserved almonds into frosting on sides of cake. Refrigerate cake, covered with inverted bowl, at least 4 hours before serving.

Makes 6 to 8 servings.

Fig & Nut Cake

¾ cup (180 mL) hazelnuts (about 4 ounces or 115 g)

⅔ cup (160 mL) slivered blanched almonds (about 3 ounces or 85 g)

¾ cup (180 mL) whole dried figs (about 4 ounces or 115 g)

⅓ cup (80 mL) diced candied orange peel

⅓ cup (80 mL) diced candied lemon peel

3 ounces (85 g) semisweet chocolate

3 large eggs

½ cup (125 mL) sugar

1¼ cups (310 mL) all-purpose flour

1¾ teaspoons (9 mL) baking powder

¾ teaspoon (4 mL) salt

1. Heat oven to 350°F (180°C). Place hazelnuts in small baking pan. Bake until toasted, 12 to 15 minutes; let cool slightly. Rub a few hazelnuts at a time between palms of hands to remove as much of the skins as possible.

2. Coarsely chop hazelnuts, almonds, figs and candied orange and lemon peels. Finely chop chocolate. Combine nuts, figs, peels and chocolate in medium bowl; mix well.

3. Heat oven to 300°F (150°C). Grease an 8 × 4 × 2½-inch (20 × 10 × 6.5 cm) loaf pan.

4. Combine eggs and sugar in large mixer bowl. Beat at high speed until mixture is very pale yellow and thick and fluffy, at least 5 minutes. Add nut mixture to egg mixture. Gently fold in.

5. Combine flour, baking powder and salt in sieve. Sift half the flour mixture over egg mixture and gently fold in; repeat with remaining flour mixture. Spoon batter into prepared pan; spread top even. Bake until top of loaf is deep golden brown and center is firm to the touch, 1 hour to 1 hour and 10 minutes. Cool loaf in pan on wire rack 5 minutes. Remove loaf from pan; cool completely on wire rack, at least 4 hours, before cutting. To serve, cut into slices.

Makes 12 to 16 servings.

Siena Cake

¾ cup (180 mL) whole blanched almonds (about 4 ounces or 115 g)

¾ cup (180 mL) hazelnuts (about 4 ounces or 115 g)

⅓ cup (80 mL) chopped candied or dried apricots

⅓ cup (80 mL) chopped candied pineapple

3 tablespoons (45 mL) each diced candied orange peel and candied lemon peel

⅔ cup (160 mL) all-purpose flour

2 tablespoons (30 mL) unsweetened cocoa

1½ teaspoons (7 mL) ground cinnamon

½ teaspoon (2 mL) ground nutmeg

¼ teaspoon (1 mL) ground coriander

2 ounces (60 g) semisweet chocolate

½ cup (125 mL) honey

⅓ cup (80 mL) granulated sugar

Powdered sugar

1. Heat oven to 350°F (180°C). Place almonds and hazelnuts

each in a separate small baking pan. Bake nuts until light brown, 7 to 10 minutes for almonds and 12 to 15 minutes for hazelnuts. Let nuts cool slightly. Rub a few hazelnuts at a time between palms of hands to remove as much of the skins as possible. Chop almonds and hazelnuts coarsely.

2. Combine nuts with apricots, pineapple, and orange and lemon peels in large bowl. Sift flour, cocoa, cinnamon, nutmeg and coriander together over nut mixture; mix well.

3. Grease an 8-inch (20 cm) round cake pan. Line bottom of pan with circle of parchment or waxed paper cut to fit. Line sides of pan with strip of paper cut to fit. Grease paper.

4. Heat oven to 325°F (160°C). Melt chocolate in top of double boiler over simmering water. Remove pan from water. Let stand at room temperature.

5. Combine honey and granulated sugar in small heavy saucepan. Cook over medium-low heat until sugar is dissolved. Brush down sides of pan with wet pastry brush to dissolve any sugar crystals. Heat syrup to boiling; reduce heat to medium-low. Simmer uncovered without stirring until syrup registers 240°F (115°C) on candy thermometer (until drops of syrup form soft balls in glass of cold water), about 5 minutes. Immediately remove from heat. Add syrup, then chocolate to nut mixture; stir to mix well.

6. Spoon batter into prepared pan; spread top even. Bake 35 minutes. Cool cake in pan on wire rack 20 minutes. Carefully remove cake from pan; remove and discard paper. Cool cake completely on wire rack. Wrap cake tightly in aluminum foil; let stand at room temperature at least 24 hours before cutting. Cake will keep well, tightly wrapped, for 2 to 3 weeks. To serve, sift powdered sugar over top of cake; cut into very thin wedges.

Makes 16 servings.

Panettone Cake

¾ cup (180 mL) milk
½ cup (125 mL) plus 3 tablespoons (45 mL) unsalted butter
½ cup (125 mL) plus 1 teaspoon (15 mL) granulated sugar
1 teaspoon (5 mL) salt
1 package (¼ ounce or 7 g) plus 1 teaspoon (5 mL) active dry yeast
¼ cup (60 mL) very warm water (105°F to 115°F or 40°C to 46°C)
2 large eggs
3 large egg yolks
5¾ cups (1430 mL) all-purpose flour
2 ounces (60 g) candied pineapple
1 tablespoon (15 mL) diced candied orange peel
1 tablespoon (15 mL) diced candied lemon peel
1 cup (250 mL) golden raisins
⅓ cup (80 mL) pine nuts (pignolias)
2 teaspoons (10 mL) grated lemon peel
Powdered sugar

1. Heat milk, ½ cup (125 mL) of the butter, ½ cup (125 mL) of the granulated sugar and the salt in small saucepan until butter is melted; transfer to large bowl and cool to luke-warm. Sprinkle yeast and remaining 1 teaspoon (5 mL) granulated sugar over the very warm water in small bowl; stir until yeast is dissolved. Let stand in warm place until bubbly, about 5 minutes. Whisk eggs and egg yolks into cooled milk mixture. Stir in 2 cups (500 mL) of the flour; beat 1 minute. Whisk in yeast mixture. Gradually stir in 2½ cups (625 mL) of the remaining flour to form soft dough. Beat 1 minute.

2. Finely chop candied pineapple and candied orange and lemon peels; stir into dough. Stir raisins, pine nuts, and grated lemon peel into dough. Beat until dough is very elastic, 2 to 3 minutes. Cover bowl with kitchen towel; let dough rise in warm place until doubled, 1 to 1½ hours.

3. Spread remaining flour on kneading surface. Spoon

dough onto flour; knead in enough flour with spatula to make dough manageable. Knead with hands, working in as much flour as needed, until dough is smooth and elastic, 5 to 8 minutes. Let rise covered in greased bowl in warm place until doubled, 45 to 60 minutes.

4. If making 2 medium cakes, grease each of two 2-pound (900 g) coffee cans with ½ table-spoon (7 mL) of the remaining butter. If making 1 large cake, fold a 28 × 18-inch (70 × 45 cm) piece of heavy-duty aluminum foil lengthwise in thirds. Fit foil strip around inside of 8-inch (20 cm) springform pan; secure with paper clip. Grease bottom of pan and inside of foil with 1 tablespoon (15 mL) of the remaining butter.

5. Punch down dough. Divide dough in half if making

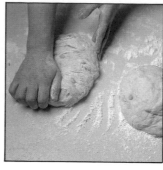

2 cakes. Knead briefly on floured surface to distribute air bubbles. Shape dough into smooth ball(s); place in pre-pared pan(s). Let rise covered in warm place until doubled, 45 to 60 minutes.

6. Heat oven to 400°F (200°C). Melt remaining 2 tablespoons (30 mL) butter in small sauce-pan. Cut shallow cross in top(s) of cake(s); brush top(s) with melted butter. Bake 10 minutes. Reduce oven setting to 325°F (160°C). Bake until deep golden brown, 30 to 35 minutes longer for medium cakes, 45 to 50 minutes longer for large cake. Cool in pan(s) on wire rack 10 minutes. Remove cake(s) from pan(s). Cool completely on wire rack, at least 6 hours, before cutting. Dust top(s) with powdered sugar through a sieve just before serving.

Makes 1 large cake or 2 medium cakes.

Almond Cookies

8 ounces (225 g) whole
  blanched almonds (about
  1½ cups or 375 mL)
1 tablespoon (15 mL)
  all-purpose flour
1 teaspoon (5 mL) grated
  lemon peel
1 large egg white, at room
  temperature
¼ cup (60 mL) sugar
1 tablespoon (15 mL) honey
1 large egg white
⅓ cup (80 mL) sugar
⅛ teaspoon (0.5 mL) vanilla

1. Heat oven to 300°F (150°C). Lightly grease 1 large baking sheet. Finely grind almonds in food processor or blender. Measure finely ground almonds; you need 2 cups (500 mL). Mix almonds, flour and lemon peel in medium bowl.

2. Beat 1 egg white in small mixer bowl until soft peaks form. Gradually beat in ¼ cup (60 mL) sugar; add honey. Continue beating until sugar is completely dissolved. Add to almond mixture; stir until thoroughly mixed. Measure out all the dough by tablespoonfuls (15 mL) onto plate or waxed paper before shaping.

3. To shape cookies: Roll each piece of dough lightly between palms to form an even, 2-inch- (5 cm) long log; press ends and top to flatten slightly. Place logs on prepared baking sheet, 1 inch (2.5 cm) apart. Bake until very light brown, 15 to 18 minutes.

4. While cookies are baking, lightly beat remaining 1 egg white in a cup. Combine 1 teaspoon (5 mL) of the egg white, the ⅓ cup (80 mL) sugar and the vanilla in small bowl; mix thoroughly.

5. Cool cookies on baking sheet on wire rack 3 minutes. Then brush tops of cookies lightly with remaining beaten egg white. Top each warm cookie with ½ teaspoon (2 mL) of the sugar-egg mixture; press lightly with back of spoon to cover top evenly. Cool cookies completely; the topping will harden.

Makes about 20 cookies.

Amaretti

7 ounces (200 g) whole
  blanched almonds (about
  1⅓ cups or 330 mL)
1 cup (250 mL) sugar
2 large egg whites
½ teaspoon (2 mL) vanilla
4 drops almond extract
30 to 35 whole blanched
  almonds

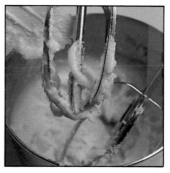

1. Heat oven to 375°F (190°C). Generously grease 2 large baking sheets; dust lightly with flour and tap off excess. Fit pastry bag with ½-inch (1.5 cm) plain tube.

2. Grind the 7 ounces (200 g) almonds in food processor or blender to medium-fine texture. Combine the ground almonds, sugar, unbeaten egg whites, vanilla and the almond extract in large mixer bowl.

3. Beat almond mixture on low speed until mixed. Then beat on medium speed until slightly thickened, 3 to 4 minutes. Let mixture stand 5 minutes. (Batter should be quite thick, as in photo. If not, grind a few of the 30 to 35 whole almonds and stir them into batter.)

4. Spoon batter into pastry bag. Pipe onto baking sheets in 1¼-inch (3 cm) rounds, 1½ inches (4 cm) apart. For garnish, lightly press whole almond in center of each. Bake until tops are light brown, 12 to 15 minutes. Immediately remove amaretti from baking sheets with metal spatula to wire racks. Cool completely. Amaretti will keep in tightly covered container for several weeks.

Makes about 30 cookies.

Florentines

¼ cup (60 mL) sliced
   blanched almonds
¼ cup (60 mL) walnuts
5 red candied cherries
1 tablespoon (15 mL) golden
   or dark raisins
1 tablespoon (15 mL) diced
   candied lemon peel
½ ounce (15 g) preserved
   ginger or 1 tablespoon
   (15 mL) crystallized
   ginger
¼ cup (60 mL) unsalted
   butter
¼ cup (60 mL) sugar
1 tablespoon (15 mL)
   whipping cream
3 tablespoons (45 mL) all-
   purpose flour
4 ounces (115 g) semisweet
   chocolate

3. Combine butter, sugar and cream in small heavy saucepan. Cook uncovered over medium heat, stirring constantly, until sugar is dissolved and mixture boils. Continue cooking and stirring 1 minute. Remove from heat. Stir in nuts, fruits and ginger. Add flour; stir to mix well.

oven to wire rack. If cookies have spread unevenly, push in edges with metal spatula to round out the shape. Cool cookies until firm enough to remove from sheet, about 1 minute, then quickly but carefully remove cookies with wide metal spatula. Cool completely on wire racks.

1. Grind almonds in blender or food processor until very fine, or chop very fine with knife. Very finely chop walnuts, cherries, raisins, lemon peel and ginger with a knife.

2. Heat oven to 350°F (180°C). Grease 2 large baking sheets.

4. Spoon batter onto prepared baking sheets. Use 1 teaspoon (5 mL) batter per cookie, 4 cookies per sheet, spacing them far apart to allow for spreading.

5. Bake cookies, 1 baking sheet at a time, until deep brown, 8 to 10 minutes. Remove baking sheet from

6. Heat water in bottom of double boiler to simmering; remove from heat. Chop chocolate fine; place in top of double boiler and place over the water. Stir chocolate just until melted, then immediately remove from water. Let chocolate cool slightly. Turn cookies over; spread chocolate on bottoms. Place cookies, chocolate-side up, on waxed paper-lined tray or baking sheet; let stand until chocolate is almost but not quite set. Score chocolate in zig-zag pattern with tines of fork. Let stand until completely set. If chocolate does not harden at room temperature, refrigerate until firm.

Makes about 2 dozen cookies.

Sicilian Creams

1¾ cups (430 mL) all-purpose
   flour
2 teaspoons (10 mL) baking
   powder
¾ teaspoon (4 mL) salt
¼ cup (60 mL) unsalted
   butter, cold
½ cup (125 mL) granulated
   sugar
1 large egg
¼ cup (60 mL) milk
1 teaspoon (5 mL) grated
   lemon peel
1 teaspoon (5 mL) vanilla
⅔ cup (160 mL) whipping
   cream
1 tablespoon (15 mL) water
1 tablespoon (15 mL) fruit- or
   nut-flavored liqueur
2 tablespoons (30 mL)
   powdered sugar

1. Mix flour, baking powder and salt in medium bowl; cut in butter with 2 knives or pastry cutter until mixture resembles fine crumbs. Add granulated sugar; mix well. Lightly beat egg in small bowl; stir in milk, lemon peel and vanilla. Pour egg mixture into flour mixture; stir to form a soft, pliable dough.

2. Knead dough on well-floured surface a few times to form smooth soft dough. Shape into 1-inch- (2.5 cm) thick disc; refrigerate wrapped in plastic 30 minutes.

3. Heat oven to 350°F (180°C). Lightly grease one large baking sheet. Roll out dough on lightly floured surface to ⅜-inch (1 cm) thickness. Cut out circles of dough with 2-inch (5 cm) round cutter dipped in flour. Place circles on baking sheet. Gather dough trimmings into ball; flatten ball, roll out and cut out more circles. Bake until light golden brown, 15 to 20 minutes. Transfer cookies from baking sheet to wire rack; cool completely.

4. Beat cream in small mixer bowl until stiff. Mix water and liqueur in cup. Cut cookies horizontally in half with thin serrated knife. Brush cut sides of cookie tops with diluted liqueur. Spoon 1 tablespoon (15 mL) whipped cream in center of each cookie bottom; press cookie tops onto cream. Sift powdered sugar over cookies through a sieve. Let stand at cool room temperature at least 30 minutes before serving.

Makes about 20 cookies.

Anise Cookies

4 ounces (115 g) whole
   blanched almonds (about
   ¾ cup or 180 mL)
2¼ cups (560 mL) all-purpose
   flour
1 teaspoon (5 mL) baking
   powder
¾ teaspoon (4 mL) salt
¾ cup (180 mL) sugar
½ cup (125 mL) unsalted
   butter, at room
   temperature
3 large eggs, at room
   temperature
2 tablespoons (30 mL)
   brandy
2 teaspoons (10 mL) grated
   lemon peel
1 tablespoon (15 mL) whole
   anise seeds

1. Heat oven to 375°F (190°C). Place almonds in small baking pan. Bake until light brown, 6 to 8 minutes. Transfer almonds to plate; let cool.

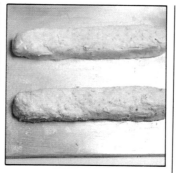

2. Chop almonds coarsely. Mix flour, baking powder and salt in small bowl. Beat sugar and butter in medium mixer bowl until light and fluffy. Add eggs, 1 at a time, beating well after each addition. Scrape down sides of bowl. Stir in brandy and the lemon peel. Add flour mixture; stir until smooth. Stir in almonds and anise seeds. Refrigerate dough covered 1 hour to firm and to blend flavors.

3. Heat oven to 375°F (190°C). Grease 1 large baking sheet. Divide dough in half. Spoon half the dough in a row lengthwise on one side of baking sheet; spread top and sides even with spatula or back of spoon, forming a 12 × 2-inch (30 × 5 cm) log. Dough will be fairly soft. Pat surface smooth with lightly floured fingertips. Repeat with remaining half of dough to form second log. Bake until logs are light golden brown, 20 to 25 minutes. (Do not turn oven off.) Cool logs completely on baking sheet on wire rack.

4. Reduce oven setting to 350°F (180°C). Cut logs diagonally with serrated knife into ½-inch (1.5 cm) thick slices. Place slices flat in single layer on 2 ungreased baking sheets. Bake 8 minutes. Turn slices over, bake until cut surfaces are light brown and cookies are dry, 10 to 12 minutes longer. Remove cookies from baking sheets to wire racks; cool completely. Cookies will keep for several weeks in tightly covered container.

Makes about 4 dozen cookies.

Custard Rum Torta

6 large eggs, at room
temperature
¾ cup (180 mL) plus ½ cup
(125 mL) granulated sugar
¾ teaspoon (4 mL) salt
1¼ cups (310 mL) all-purpose
flour
⅓ cup (80 mL) cornstarch
3½ cups (875 mL) milk
2 large egg yolks
2 tablespoons (30 mL) butter
2 teaspoons (10 mL) vanilla
2 pints (1 L) fresh
strawberries
6 tablespoons (90 mL) golden
rum
¼ cup (60 mL) powdered
sugar
2 pints (1 L) whipping cream
Light corn syrup, if desired

1. For cake: Heat oven to 350°F
(180°C). Grease and flour 10-
inch (25 cm) springform pan.
Beat eggs in large mixer bowl
at high speed until foamy
throughout. Beat in ¾ cup (180
mL) of the granulated sugar, 2
tablespoons (30 mL) at a time,
beating well after each addition. Beat 3 minutes longer.
Beat in ¼ teaspoon (1 mL) of
the salt. Sift a third of the flour
over egg mixture through
sieve; fold in. Repeat until all
flour has been incorporated.
Pour batter into prepared
springform pan; spread top
even. Bake until wooden pick
inserted in center is with-
drawn clean, about 40 minutes. Cool cake in pan on wire
rack 10 minutes. Loosen edge
of cake with tip of knife;
remove cake from pan. Cool
cake completely on rack. Clean
pan.

2. For custard: Combine
remaining ½ cup (125 mL)
granulated sugar, the cornstarch and remaining ½ teaspoon (2 mL) salt in large
saucepan; mix thoroughly. Stir
in milk until smooth. Cook
uncovered, stirring frequently,
over medium heat to boiling.
Boil, stirring constantly, 3 minutes; remove from heat. Whisk
egg yolks in small bowl; gradually whisk in about 1 cup (250
mL) of the hot milk mixture.
Gradually whisk egg yolk mixture into remaining milk mix-

ture in pan. Cook over very
low heat, stirring constantly, 1
minute. Immediately transfer
custard to medium bowl. Cut
butter into 6 pieces; add to custard and stir until melted. Stir
in vanilla. Cover surface of
custard with waxed paper; let
cool completely.

3. Rinse and drain strawberries. Reserve 8 whole berries,
wrapped in plastic, in
refrigerator for garnish. Hull
and thinly slice remaining
berries.

4. To assemble dessert: Cut
cake horizontally with thin
serrated knife into 3 even layers. Brush top of each layer
with 2 tablespoons (30 mL) of
the rum. Place one cake layer
in bottom of the cleaned

springform pan. Top with half
the custard; spread even.
Arrange half the berry slices
over custard in single layer.
Top with second cake layer;
spread with remaining custard
and top with remaining berries. Cover with third cake
layer. Refrigerate covered at
least 12 hours.

5. About 45 minutes before
serving, sift powdered sugar.
Beat cream with powdered
sugar in large mixer bowl until
stiff. Spoon 2 cups (500 mL) of
the whipped cream into pastry
bag fitted with large star tube;
reserve in refrigerator. Remove
sides of springform pan from
dessert; place dessert on serving plate (do not remove bottom of springform). Spread
remaining whipped cream
evenly and smoothly on sides
and top of dessert. Pipe
reserved cream in border on
top of dessert. Refrigerate 30
minutes before serving.

6. Just before serving, garnish
dessert with reserved whole
berries; brush berries with
corn syrup. Cut dessert into
wedges to serve.

Makes 10 servings.

Cassata

First Layer
2 large eggs, separated
½ cup (125 mL) sifted
  powdered sugar
½ cup (125 mL) whipping
  cream
4 drops almond extract

Second Layer
2 tablespoons (30 mL)
  unsweetened cocoa
1½ tablespoons (22 mL) cold
  water
2 ounces (60 g) semisweet
  chocolate
2 large eggs, separated
½ cup (125 mL) sifted
  powdered sugar
½ cup (125 mL) whipping
  cream

Third Layer
⅓ cup (80 mL) sliced
  blanched almonds
6 red candied cherries
6 green candied cherries
2 ounces (60 g) candied
  pineapple
2 candied or dried apricots
1 large egg white

⅓ cup (80 mL) sifted
  powdered sugar
1 cup (250 mL) whipping
  cream
1 teaspoon (5 mL) vanilla

1. Place 9 × 3-inch (23 × 8 cm) round cake pan or 9-inch (23 cm) springform pan in freezer.

2. For first layer: Beat egg whites in large mixer bowl until soft peaks form; gradually beat in sugar. Lightly beat egg yolks in small bowl; fold into egg whites. Beat cream and almond extract in small mixer bowl until stiff; fold into egg white mixture. Pour into chilled pan; spread even. Freeze until firm, at least 1 hour.

3. For second layer: Mix cocoa and water in cup until smooth.

Melt semisweet chocolate in small bowl over hot, not simmering, water; remove from water. Whisk egg yolks into chocolate; whisk in cocoa mixture. Beat egg whites in large mixer bowl until soft peaks form; gradually beat in sugar. Beat cream in small mixer bowl until stiff. Fold cream into egg whites, then fold in chocolate mixture. Pour over first layer in pan; spread even. Freeze until firm, at least 1 hour.

4. For third layer: Heat oven to 350°F (180°C). Bake almonds in small baking pan until light brown, 6 to 8 minutes; let coo Chop red and green cherrie pineapple and apricots. Bea egg white in small mixer bov until soft peaks form; gradu ally beat in sugar. Beat crear and vanilla in large mixer bov until stiff; fold in egg white Add almonds and fruits; st gently until evenly dis tributed. Pour mixture ove chocolate layer in pan; sprea even. Freeze covered unt very firm throughout, at least hours. To serve, unmold des sert; cut into wedges.

Makes 8 to 10 servings.

Lemon Granita

½ cup (125 mL) sweet or dry
  fruity white wine
½ cup (125 mL) water
½ cup (125 mL) sugar
½ cup (125 mL) strained
  fresh lemon juice
1 large egg white, at room
  temperature

1. Measure wine and water into small saucepan; add sugar. Cook over medium-high heat, stirring frequently, until sugar is dissolved and syrup boils. Cover pan; boil 1 minute. Uncover pan; adjust heat to maintain simmer. Simmer without stirring 10 minutes. Remove from heat. Refrigerate uncovered until syrup is completely cooled, about 30 minutes.

2. Stir lemon juice into cooled syrup. Pour into 11 × 7 × 2-inch (28 × 18 × 5 cm) metal baking pan or 9-inch (23 cm) round cake pan. Freeze 30 minutes. Quickly stir mixture with fork breaking up ice crystals and mixing until texture is even. Freeze until firm throughout but not solid, about 30 minutes longer. Meanwhile, place medium bowl in freezer to chill.

3. Beat egg white in smal mixer bowl until stiff but no dry peaks form. Transfe lemon ice mixture from pan t chilled bowl. Working quickly beat ice with whisk or for until smooth. Add egg white mix well. Quickly return mix ture to pan; spread even Freeze 15 minutes. Stir quickly with fork; cover pan with foi Freeze until very firm before serving, at least 3 hours. Serve granita with berries and/o butter cookies, if desired.

Makes 4 servings.

Zabaglione

5 large egg yolks
¼ cup (60 mL) sugar
½ cup (125 mL) marsala
¼ cup (60 mL) dry white
  wine

1. Place egg yolks in top of double boiler; add sugar. Beat with portable electric mixer or rotary beaters until mixture is pale yellow and creamy.

2. Place top of double boiler over simmering water over low heat. Gradually beat half the marsala into egg yolk mixture. Beat 1 minute. Gradually beat in remaining marsala and the white wine.

3. Reduce heat to very low; continue cooking custard over

gently simmering water, bea ing constantly and scrapin bottom and sides of pan fr quently, until mixture is fluf and thick enough to form so mounds when dropped fro beaters, 6 to 10 minutes. Watc very carefully and do not ove cook or custard will curdl Immediately remove top double boiler from wate Whisk custard briefly; pou into individual serving dishe Serve at once with fruit and/c cookies, if desired.

Makes 4 servings.

Cannoli

1¾ cups (430 mL) all-purpose
  flour
2 tablespoons (30 mL)
  granulated sugar
2 teaspoons (10 mL) grated
  lemon peel
2 tablespoons (30 mL) butter,
  cold
1 large egg, cold
6 tablespoons (90 mL)
  marsala
2 pounds (900 g) ricotta
  cheese
1½ cups (375 mL) sifted
  powdered sugar
2 teaspoons (10 mL) ground
  cinnamon
¼ cup (60 mL) diced candied
  orange peel, minced
Vegetable oil
Powdered sugar
2 ounces (60 g) semisweet
  chocolate, finely chopped

1. Mix flour, granulated sugar and 1 teaspoon (5 mL) of the lemon peel in medium bowl; cut in butter with 2 knives or pastry cutter until mixture resembles fine crumbs. Beat egg and marsala in small bowl; add to flour mixture. Stir with fork to form ball. Divide dough in half; shape each piece into 1-inch- (2.5 cm) thick square. Refrigerate wrapped in plastic at least 1 hour.

2. For filling: Beat ricotta cheese in large mixer bowl on medium speed until smooth. Add 1½ cups (375 mL) powdered sugar and the cinnamon; beat on high speed 3 minutes. Add orange peel and remaining 1 teaspoon (5 mL) lemon peel to cheese mixture; stir to mix well: Refrigerate covered until serving time.

3. Heat 1½ inches (4 cm) oil in large saucepan to 325°F (160°C). Working with 1 piece of dough at a time, roll out on lightly floured surface to ¹⁄₁₆ inch (2 mm) thickness. Cut dough with knife into 4 × 3-inch (10 × 8 cm) rectangles. Wrap each rectangle around a

metal cannoli form or around uncooked cannelloni pasta shell (shown in photo). Brush one edge of rectangle lightly with water; overlap with other edge and press firmly to seal.

4. Fry 2 or 3 cannoli at a time turning once, until ligh brown, 1 to 1½ minutes Remove with tongs to pape towel-lined rack; let stand unt cool enough to handle. Care fully remove fried pastrie from cannoli forms or past shells; cool completely. Re serve pastries uncovered a room temperature.

5. When ready to serve spoon cheese filling into pastr bag filled with large plai tube. Pipe about ¼ cup (60 mL filling into each reserve pastry shell.* Roll cannoli i powdered sugar to coat. Di filling at ends of cannoli int chocolate. Arrange cannoli o serving plate. Dust lightly wit powdered sugar through sieve.

Makes 18 to 20.

*Note:*Do not fill cannoli ahea of time or pastry will becom soggy.

Index